W9-CKF-453

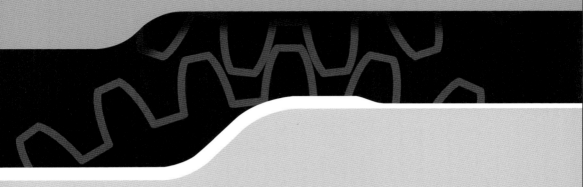

Technology Through the Ages

The Scientific Revolution

609
SCi

BROWN
BEAR
BOOKS

Published by Brown Bear Books Limited

An imprint of:
The Brown Reference Group Ltd
68 Topstone Road
Redding
Connecticut 06896
USA
www.brownreference.com

© 2009 The Brown Reference Group Ltd

ISBN: 978-1-933834-85-6

Editorial Director: Lindsey Lowe
Managing Editor: Tim Harris
Project Director: Graham Bateman
Editors: Briony Ryles, Derek Hall
Designer: Steve McCurdy
Picture Research: Steve McCurdy

Library of Congress Cataloging-in-Publication Data available upon request

Picture Credits

Cover Image
The Iron Bridge over the River Severn, England (Shutterstock, Tom Curtis)

Shutterstock:
37 Knud Nielsen; 38 Anyka.

Photos.com:
7; 8; 11; 14; 17; 20; 22–23; 27; 28–29; 31; 35; 42–43; 44; 45; 47; 50; 52–53; 55; 57; 58–59; 60–61; 62; 64–65; 67; 69; 73; 76; 79; 87

Artwork © The Brown Reference Group Ltd

The Brown Reference Group Ltd has made every effort to trace copyright holders of the pictures used in this book. Anyone having claims to ownership not identified above is invited to contact The Brown Reference Group Ltd.

Printed in the United States of America

Contents

Introduction

Technology through the Ages forms part of the Curriculum Connections project. This six-volume set describes the story of scientific discovery from the earliest use of fire and the development of the wheel through to space travel, modern computing, and the Human Genome Project. Each volume in the set covers a major historical period, ranging from prehistory up to modern times.

Within each volume there are two types of article:

In-depth articles form the core of the work, and focus on scientific discoveries and technological progress of particular note, giving background to the topic, information about the people involved, and explanations of how the discoveries or inventions have been put to use. Each article focuses on a particular step forward that originated within this period, but the articles often extend back into the history of the topic or forward to later developments to help give further context to each subject. Boxed features add to the information, often explaining scientific principles.

Within each article there are two key aids to learning, which are to be found in color bars located in the margins of each page:

Curriculum Context sidebars indicate to the reader that a subject has particular relevance to certain key State and National Science and Technology Education Standards up to Grade 12.

Glossary sidebars define key words within the text.

Timeline articles, to be found at the end of each volume, list year-by-year scientific discoveries, inventions, technological advances, and key dates of exploration. For each period, the timelines are divided into horizontal bands that each focus on a particular theme of technology or science.

A summary *Glossary* lists the key terms defined in the volume, and the *Index* lists people and major topics covered. Fully captioned *Illustrations* play a major role in the set, and include early prints and paintings, contemporary photographs, artwork reconstructions, and explanatory diagrams.

About this Volume

In this volume (*The Scientific Revolution—1625 through 1825*) we cover a period when great scientific progress was made, which led in its turn to the massive technological innovations of the Industrial Revolution. The 17th and 18th centuries were a time of experimenters, not just thinkers. Galileo developed his ideas about pendulums by using his pulse rate to time the swings of a chandelier in Pisa Cathedral, and is said to have tested his theory about falling objects by dropping cannonballs from the Leaning Tower of Pisa. Isaac Newton used a prism to split white light into a spectrum, and developed theories on gravitation. In America, Benjamin Franklin experimented with lightning as well as inventing bifocal eyeglasses and a nonsmoking wood-burning stove. In biology, scientists came to recognize that fossils are the remains of long-dead plants and animals—but why did fossils become extinct? The answer to that question was to come in the 19th century with the theories of Charles Darwin.

Elsewhere, the production of cheaper iron using coke instead of charcoal (introduced by Abraham Darby), and the invention of the steam engine by James Watt, paved the way for the Industrial Revolution. Steam engines became the workhorses of the new factories that spread across Europe and North America, powering pumps and many other kinds of machines, and heralding the farming revolution that was needed to feed growing urban populations. But the steam engine really came into its own when used in transportation. While the late 18th century saw the first trials using steam to power ships, more significantly, in 1903, the first steam locomotive was built—and with this invention, railroads were born. Meanwhile in laboratories, scientists like Michael Faraday were taking the first steps on a path to a new source of energy and power—the age of electricity was dawning.

Telescopes

The first lenses were used mainly as magnifying glasses. They were convex (converging) lenses, curving outward on each side, that produced enlarged images of nearby objects. But scientists and astronomers needed to have an enlarged image of distant objects. The telescope fulfilled this need.

Curriculum Context

Students are expected to research and describe the contributions of scientists.

Hans Lippershey (c.1570–c.1619), the German-born Dutch eyeglass maker, made his first telescope in 1608. He sold his invention to the Dutch government for use by the military, but they would not grant him a patent because other people laid claim to the invention. News of the device—which would be described today as a refracting telescope—reached the Italian scientist Galileo Galilei (1564–1642), who immediately made his own telescopes to study the skies. Among his many discoveries were sunspots, craters on the Moon, and the four major moons of Jupiter.

Another contemporary astronomer, the German Johannes Kepler (1571–1630), explained how this type of telescope works. A concave eyepiece lens focuses an enlarged image produced by the convex object lens. He also suggested that a telescope would provide a wider field of view using two convex lenses—a design adopted by German astronomer Christopher Scheiner (1575–1650) in 1611. Called an astronomical telescope, it produces an upside-down image. For centuries afterward, images of the Moon, for instance, were always shown with "north" at the bottom.

Curriculum Context

Students should understand that light can be reflected by a mirror, refracted by a lens, or absorbed by the object.

Reducing chromatic aberration

Lenses of the time suffered from various defects, such as chromatic aberration, which results in colored fringes around images. Grinding and polishing lenses reduces aberration to some extent, as discovered by Dutch scientist Christiaan Huygens (1629–95) in 1655.

With his improved astronomical telescope he first observed the rings of Saturn.

But it was not until 1758 that Englishman John Dollond (1706–61), maker of optical and astronomical instruments, finally made an achromatic telescope. He rediscovered a method of making achromatic lenses first used in 1733 by English amateur astronomer Chester Hall (1703–71). The method, still used today, involves making a compound lens with two separate components stuck together. The second component, made of crown glass, corrects the aberrations caused

The huge reflecting telescope built by German-born English astronomer William Herschel (1738–1822) in 1789 had a focal length of over 39 feet (12 m).

The Scottish mathematician James Gregory designed the first reflecting telescope in 1663, and Isaac Newton built his own version (above) in 1668. This telescope had the eyepiece at the side. It had a 1.3-inch (3.3-cm) mirror, and magnified objects about 40 times.

by the first component, which is made out of flint glass. It works because the two types of glass bend light rays in slightly different ways.

Another method of avoiding chromatic aberration involved using lenses with only slight curvature, and therefore a long focal length (the length of the telescope's light path from the main mirror or object lens to the focal point—the location of the eyepiece). This meant making telescopes very long. Telescopes measuring 33 feet (10 m) long were common, and by 1650 the Polish amateur astronomer Johannes Hevelius (1611–87) had constructed a telescope 148 feet (45 m) long. These so-called aerial telescopes employed only a skeleton tube hanging from a mast, and were aimed using a system of ropes and pulleys.

Reflecting telescopes

A better way to view images is with a reflecting telescope that uses mirrors instead of lenses, because mirrors do not cause chromatic aberration. James Gregory (1638–75), a Scottish mathematician and inventor, realized this in 1663 when he published a design for a telescope that had a small, curved secondary mirror to reflect the light back through a hole in the primary mirror to an eyepiece. English scientist Robert Hooke (1635–1703) later improved the design. Other types of reflecting telescope were built— by English scientist Isaac Newton (1642–1727) in 1668, and by French priest Laurent Cassegrain (1629–93) in 1672. (The complex Cassegrainian design was not perfected until 1740 by Scottish optician James Short, 1710–68.) In 1857, French physicist Léon Foucault (1819–68) devised a method of silvering glass to make curved mirrors. They were easier to manufacture, and could be resilvered if accidentally damaged. Since then astronomical telescopes have been made larger and more powerful—it is far easier to make a big mirror than it is to make a big lens.

Refracting and Reflecting Telescopes

One kind of refracting telescope is the type originally designed by Galileo in 1609. It uses two lenses and produces an upright image. Small versions can be paired to form binoculars. Of the two reflecting designs shown below, the Newtonian has the eyepiece at the side, which can be inconvenient in a large telescope.

The Cassegrainian telescope has the eyepiece at the lower end, where it is easier to use.

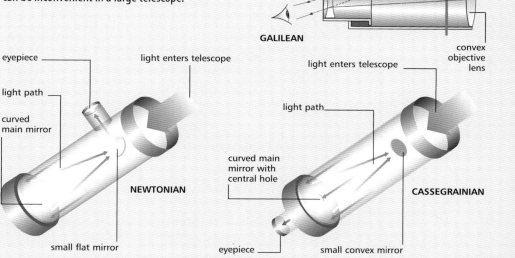

concave eyepiece lens

final image

GALILEAN

convex objective lens

eyepiece

light enters telescope

light path

curved main mirror

NEWTONIAN

small flat mirror

light enters telescope

light path

curved main mirror with central hole

CASSEGRAINIAN

eyepiece

small convex mirror

Today's largest refracting telescope, using lenses, has a diameter of about 40 inches (100 cm). It is sited at the Yerkes Observatory near Chicago, and was built in 1897. The mirror in the Hale reflecting telescope at Mount Palomar, California, commissioned in 1948, has a diameter of 16.6 feet (5 m). Even larger telescopes have mirrors made up of many smaller hexagonal segments that fit together like a honeycomb. A computer controls the segments, and their positions can be altered to adjust the focus of the mirror. The largest telescopes of this type, with 36 segments each, have mirrors 33 feet (10 m) across. Two are situated at the Keck Observatory in Hawaii.

Curriculum Context

Students should know the concept of light and optics.

The pendulum clock and Galileo

The Chinese constructed the first mechanical clocks, which were in effect large, slowly turning waterwheels made of wood. Metal clocks powered by falling weights date from the 1300s, but they were unreliable and inaccurate. What was needed was a way of closely regulating the mechanism, and that arrived in the 1600s as the first practical application of the pendulum.

The Italian scientist Galileo Galilei (1564–1642) was born in Pisa in northern Italy, the son of a distinguished musician. He went to Florence to be educated at a monastery school; and when he was only 17 years old, he began attending the University of Pisa to study medicine. He soon switched to mathematics and philosophy, but left school in 1585 without a degree and began working as a teacher.

Swinging pendulums

It was in 1582, however, while attending a service in Pisa Cathedral, that Galileo noticed the regular movements of a lamp swinging in the air draft above his head. He made his own simple pendulum—for that is what the swinging lamp was—consisting of a weight at the end of a length of string, and then timed its swings. In those days stopwatches did not exist, and he used the beat of his own pulse to time the swings.

Galileo demonstrated that a pendulum always swings at a constant rate. He also proved that the rate of swing depends only on the length of the pendulum, and not on the size of the weight swinging at its end. In mathematical terms the time taken for one swing is proportional to the square root of the length of the pendulum. For example, a pendulum 39 inches (99 cm) long takes one second to make one swing (forward and back). So, if a pendulum of that length keeps swinging, it can mark off seconds of time.

The pendulum clock

Galileo realized that pendulums could thus be used to regulate mechanical clocks. In 1641—a year before he died—he instructed his son Vincenzo (1606–49) how to make a clock regulated by a pendulum. Vincenzo did not complete the job, however, and it was not until 1657 that the first pendulum clock appeared. It was designed by the Dutch scientist Christiaan Huygens (1629–95) a year before, and constructed by clockmaker Salomon Coster in The Hague. It kept time to within five minutes a day, and was much more accurate than any earlier clocks.

Clock pendulums use a metal rod rather than a piece of string. However, the metal of the rod does not stay

As well as his observations about pendulums, Galileo was also famous for his work in other fields of science, including astronomy. In this print he is demonstrating his telescope to some colleagues.

Falling Objects

According to the teachings of the ancient Greek philosopher Aristotle, a heavy object, such as a large rock, must fall faster than a light one, such as a pebble. This assumption was based on logic, and reflected the logical approach of the Greek philosophers. Galileo was not so sure. He put the theory to the test. The story goes that he dropped a pair of cannon balls of unequal size from the top of the Leaning Tower of Pisa. He showed that the two fell at exactly the same speed because they both hit the ground at the same time. He also tried to demonstrate that they fell at a constant acceleration. (Acceleration is the rate at which speed changes.) The illustration shows the results he would have obtained had he been able to measure acceleration. As an object falls farther, it moves faster, but the acceleration is constant—32 feet (9.8 m) per second per second. This is now known as the acceleration of free fall, or the acceleration due to gravity.

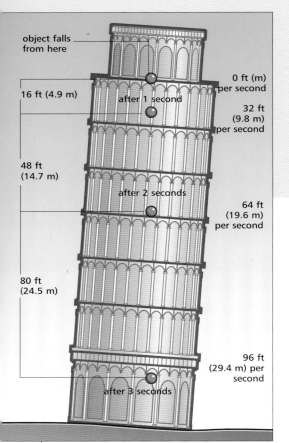

object falls from here

16 ft (4.9 m)

after 1 second

0 ft (m) per second

32 ft (9.8 m) per second

48 ft (14.7 m)

after 2 seconds

64 ft (19.6 m) per second

80 ft (24.5 m)

96 ft (29.4 m) per second

after 3 seconds

at a constant length—a factor that is crucial for accuracy—but varies depending on temperature. The rod gets longer when it is warm, and shorter when it is cold. A clock with a one-second pendulum, for instance, needs an increase in length of just 0.0009 inches (0.025 mm) in order to lose about one second a day, and a steel rod expands by that much with a temperature rise of only 4°F (2°C).

To overcome the problem, inventors soon devised various ways of making a pendulum that kept a constant length. In 1722 English inventor George Graham (1673–1751) designed the mercury pendulum (announced in 1726), which has a glass jar of mercury as the pendulum's weight. When the pendulum expands downward because of a rise in temperature, the change is counterbalanced by the upward expansion of the mercury in the jar. Another solution, the gridiron pendulum, was invented by English clockmaker John Harrison (1693–1776) in 1728. His design has a grid of alternate brass and steel rods. Brass expands more than steel, so the expansion of the brass compensates for the lesser expansion of steel. A pendulum rod made of concentric tubes of iron and zinc achieves a similar result. Today pendulum rods are made from invar, an alloy of iron and nickel that expands very little when heated. It is also used for making measuring tapes and tuning forks, in which stable dimensions are important.

Mercury

A heavy silvery metallic element, which is the only metal that is liquid at ordinary temperatures.

Big grandfathers
Have you ever wondered why a grandfather clock (known technically as a long-case clock) is so tall? It must be long enough to house a 39-inch (99-cm) one-second pendulum, common to all such clocks. They repeatedly go tick, tock every second.

Acceleration due to gravity
Since the time of the Greek philosopher Aristotle (384–322 B.C.) people thought that the speed at which an object fell depended on its weight. As an experimental scientist Galileo put this idea to the test in about 1602. He dropped two cannon balls of different weight from the Leaning Tower of Pisa— according to tradition—and showed that they hit the ground at the same time. This experiment was repeated in front of millions of people in 1969 when a U. S. Apollo astronaut dropped a feather and a hammer on the surface of the Moon. In the absence of air resistance, the two objects reached the ground at the same time.

Curriculum Context

The curriculum requires that students understand the concepts of force, acceleration, and gravity.

Galileo and the telescope
The development of the telescope in the early 1600s stimulated Galileo's interest in astronomy. He made

The French physicist Léon Foucault (1819–68) using a device he invented, the Foucault pendulum, to demonstrate the Earth's rotation.

telescopes of his own—ever the practical scientist—and pointed them at the Moon. He made drawings recording the Moon's mountains and craters at different times during the month. He then studied Jupiter, and in 1610 announced that the planet had four moons of its own. A year later he aimed his telescope at the Sun, and noted that sometimes small black spots moved slowly across the Sun's disk. The apparent movement of sunspots also convinced him that the Sun is rotating slowly on its axis.

Clashing with the Church

Galileo's discoveries about the Sun and planets finally convinced him that the Sun is at the center of the Universe (or solar system, as we would call it), a theory that had first been published in 1543 by Polish astronomer Nicolaus Copernicus (1473–1543). But the idea went against the long-held teachings of Aristotle, who postulated an Earth-centered Universe. What was worse, the idea was contrary to the teachings of the powerful Roman Catholic church. Church officials instructed Galileo not to spread the idea, but in 1632

Curriculum Context

Students should understand that scientists are influenced by societal, cultural, and personal beliefs and ways of viewing the world.

he published it in a book. Sales of the book were banned. In 1633 Galileo was arrested by the Inquisition, taken to Rome, and under threat of torture, made to recant his "heretical" views.

Old and in failing health, Galileo was banished to his home near Florence. He went blind in 1637, possibly because of eye damage caused by looking at the Sun. He was not allowed to move around freely, although he was allowed occasional visitors. One of them was English poet John Milton (1608–74). Coincidentally, Milton also went blind—one of his best-known sonnets was "On His Blindness," published in 1645. Galileo's own failing eyesight made him bitter because he could no longer observe the Universe that had been his life's work. When he died in 1642, he was suffering from arthritis and high blood pressure. Pope Urban VIII refused to forget his feud with Galileo, and he was buried unceremoniously in the Church of Santo Croce in Florence.

Curriculum Context

Students should know that much can be learned by studying the daily lives of scientists.

The Constant Pendulum

Galileo was the first person to notice that a pendulum has a constant rate of swing. Observing a swinging lamp in Pisa Cathedral, and using his own pulse to keep time, he found that the rate of swing depends only on the length of the pendulum—it is independent of the size of the weight on the end and the angle of swing (as long as the angle is fairly small).

In modern mathematical terms the time of the swing (called its period) is proportional to the square root of the length of the pendulum. So, for a long period a very long pendulum is needed. A one-second pendulum has to be 39 inches (99 cm) in length.

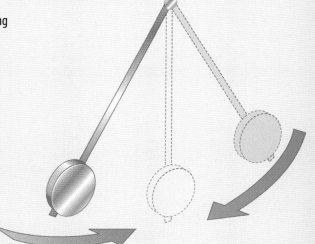

The nature of light and Isaac Newton

Early scientific studies revealed various properties of light—how it is bent by lenses, how it casts shadows, even how fast it travels—but fundamental to understanding those properties is a knowledge of the nature of light itself. In particular, does light consist of a stream of minute particles, moving like bullets from a machine gun? Or does light consist of waves capable of rippling across the vast vacuum of space?

It is clear that parallel rays of light bend as they go through a lens, and come to a focus. The concentration of the rays allows a magnifying glass to be used as a burning glass, an application known since ancient times. In 212 B.C. the Greek scientist Archimedes (*c.*287–212 B.C.) is said to have used a burning glass to destroy ships of the Roman fleet at Syracuse. The first person to measure the bending of light in this way was the Dutch mathematician Willebrord Snell (1580–1626). In 1621, he found that when a ray of light goes through a piece of glass, the angle of incidence (at which it enters the glass) is related to the angle of refraction (the angle through which it is bent) by a property of the glass now known as the refractive index.

Another mathematician, the Frenchman Pierre de Fermat (1601–65), figured out how light casts shadows. Fermat stated that it is because light always travels in straight lines—it will not "go around corners". Known as Fermat's principle, it was proposed in 1640. He also observed that light travels slower in a denser medium.

The speed of light

The first attempt to measure the speed of light was made in 1676 by Danish astronomer Ole Rømer (1644–1710). He was checking the predictions made by Italian astronomer Giovanni Cassini (1625–1712) about the timing of eclipses of Jupiter's moons (when they

Isaac Newton was one of the first people to make a scientific study of light. He believed that light travels as a stream of particles.

move out of sight behind the planet). He discovered that the eclipses seemed to happen earlier than predicted when the Earth was moving toward Jupiter, and later when the Earth was moving away from it. Rømer accounted for the differences by assuming that the light had to travel a shorter or longer distance, and that light must therefore have a finite speed, which he calculated as 140,000 miles (225,000 km) per second—about 75 percent of the actual value. It was nearly 200 years before French physicist Armand Fizeau (1819–96) obtained a more accurate value—about 5 percent too high—of 195,737 miles (315,000 km) per second.

Eclipse

An alignment between the Sun and two other celestial objects in which one body blocks the light of the Sun from the other.

Snell's Law

Snell's law is named for the Dutch mathematician Willebrord Snell (1580–1626), who discovered the phenomenon in 1621 when he was professor of mathematics at Leyden (now Leiden) University. It concerns refraction of light, which is the way a ray of light changes direction when it goes from one transparent medium to another—for example, moving from air into a block of glass. The amount of refraction depends on an optical property of the denser medium, called its refractive index. The law says that the sine of the angle of incidence divided by the sine of the angle of refraction equals the refractive index.

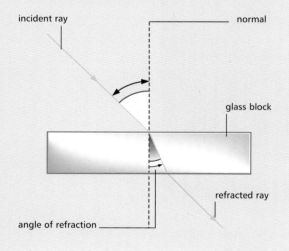

incident ray

normal

glass block

refracted ray

angle of refraction

This in turn was improved on by American physicist Albert Michelson (1852–1931) in 1882, who calculated it to be 186,325 miles (299,853 km) per second. The value that is used today is 186,288 miles (299,793 km) per second.

What is light?

In the branch of physics that we now call optics, English scientist Isaac Newton (1642–1727) allowed a narrow beam of white light from the Sun to pass through a glass prism. This split the light into a multicolored spectrum, the sequence of colors seen in a rainbow. Newton showed that white light is made up of a variety of colors. (Today we say that it is made up of many different wavelengths.)

In 1675 Newton stated that light travels as a stream of minute particles. Various physicists challenged this idea, the first being his rival Robert Hooke (1635–1703), who had already proposed the wave theory in 1665. The fact that light is refracted by glass, and the fact that it travels more slowly in water than in air, for example, were cited as evidence that it travels as waves. The final nail in the coffin of Newton's particle theory came in 1801, when English physicist Thomas Young (1773–1829) found the interference of light, a phenomenon in which white light shining through a slit is split into the colors of the rainbow.

Curriculum Context

Students should understand that light travels in waves.

At that time it could be explained only if light traveled as waves. Young published his findings in 1804.

At the beginning of the 20th century German physicist Max Planck (1858–1947) put forward his quantum theory. It postulates that all forms of energy, including light, travel in finite "packets," or quanta, similar in fact to Newton's idea. But as modern physics continued to develop, French physicist Louis de Broglie (1892–1987) suggested in 1924 that moving particles can also behave like waves, and this was soon proved to be so. Thus Newton, Hooke, and the others were all correct, and one of the great arguments of science ended.

Speed of light

The speed of light in the vacuum of free space is an important physical constant equalling 186,288 miles (299,793 km) per second.

Measuring the Speed of Light

In 1849 Armand Fizeau made the first fairly accurate measurement of the speed of light. He bounced a light ray between two mirrors 5.6 miles (9 km) apart, directing the ray between the teeth of a fast-rotating cogwheel. The returning ray went between the next pair of teeth, and then through a semisilvered mirror to the observer. He adjusted the speed of the cogwheel so that there was no flicker as the light traveled the 5.6 miles (9 km) and back. Using the wheel's speed and the distance traveled by the light, Fizeau was able to calculate the speed of light.

Albert Michelson's method of 1882 used a rotating mirror to reflect a light beam to a curved mirror 21.7 miles (35 km) away. The first mirror was rotated by an electric motor, and reflected the returning beam into an eyepiece. The speed of the motor was gradually increased until the light did not flicker. The time taken for the light to make the 44-mile (70-km) round trip could then be calculated using the rotation speed of the mirror.

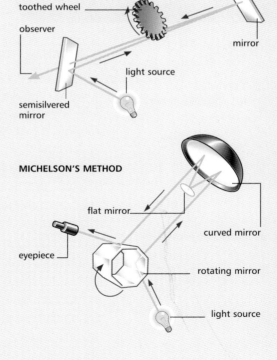

FIZEAU'S METHOD

toothed wheel

observer

mirror

light source

semisilvered mirror

MICHELSON'S METHOD

flat mirror

curved mirror

eyepiece

rotating mirror

light source

A great scientist

Isaac Newton was born in eastern England, and educated at Trinity College (Cambridge University). He received his bachelor's degree in 1665, but was forced to remain in the countryside because of the plague that raged at that time. At first he concentrated on mathematics, working out the principles of "fluxions," which were to lead to differential calculus. In 1667, Newton received a fellowship of Trinity College and became professor of mathematics in 1669. He turned his attention to what happens when objects move—what makes them start moving and what stops them. His conclusions are summed up in Newton's three laws of motion.

Isaac Newton watches an apple fall. This event led him to formulate his theory of gravity.

Discovering gravity

Newton's next contribution was to have a profound effect on the science of astronomy. It is said that he was sitting in an orchard when he saw an apple fall. Why did it fall? Newton concluded that it was attracted toward the Earth by a force, which we now call the force of gravity. He also deduced that every object behaves as if its mass were concentrated in one place, its center of gravity (now called the center of mass). Newton figured out that all objects in the Universe are affected by such gravitational forces—it is gravity that keeps the Moon in orbit around the Earth, and the Earth and other planets in orbit around the Sun. He produced a formula, the universal law of gravitation, that states the gravitational force between any two objects—two pool balls or even two stars—is equal to the product of their masses, and inversely proportional to the distance between them.

Curriculum Context

The curriculum requires that students investigate and describe applications of Newton's laws.

The distinguished English scientist Robert Hooke also devised a law of gravity in about 1678 and published his ideas a few years later. This led to a bitter dispute between the two great men.

Honored and remembered

In 1699 Newton became master of the Royal Mint. In 1703, he was elected president of the Royal Society, and two years later he was knighted by Queen Anne. As Sir Isaac Newton he continued to be showered with honors. His final tribute was a state funeral followed by a burial in Westminster Abbey, London. Newton's name lives on in the SI unit of force, which is called the newton (the force that gives 1 kilogram an acceleration of 1 meter per second per second).

Gravity

The force of attraction existing between all matter in the Universe; one of the fundamental forces of nature.

Newton's Laws

Newton formulated laws about two major topics in physics: gravity and motion. His law of gravity deals with the attractive force (gravitation) that exists between any two objects that have mass. The strength of the force depends on how close they are to each other (the nearer they are, the stronger is the force trying to pull them together), and how massive they are (the more massive they are, the stronger the force that exists between them). In mathematical terms the gravitational force is proportional to the product of the masses, and is inversely proportional to the distance between the masses.

Newton's first law of motion states that an object at rest will remain at rest (and a moving object will continue moving) unless an outside force acts on it. According to the second law, force is something that makes an object accelerate (force = mass x acceleration). The third law states that for every "action" (a force an object exerts on another) there is an equal and opposite "reaction" (exerted by the second object on the first).

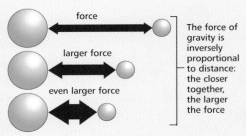

The force of gravity is inversely proportional to distance: the closer together, the larger the force

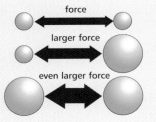

The force of gravity is proportional to the product of the masses: the larger the masses, the larger the force

The barometer and vacuums

We know that air has mass, and that atmospheric pressure results from the weight of the atmosphere pressing down on every object on Earth. But these statements have not always been taken as fact. In the 1640s, an Italian scientist named Evangelista Torricelli set out to measure air pressure; in doing so, he proved the existence of the vacuum, and invented the barometer.

Vacuum

A completely empty space in which there are no atoms or molecules of any substance.

Evangelista Torricelli (1608–47) trained as a mathematician, and in 1641 went to work as an assistant to the aged Galileo (1564–1642), who always maintained that there is no such thing as a vacuum.

In 1645, aided by his own assistant Vincenzo Viviani (1622–1703), Torricelli took a 6.6-foot (2-m) glass tube, sealed at one end, and filled it with mercury. Keeping his thumb over the open end, he upended the tube in a dish full of mercury, and then removed his thumb. Some of the mercury ran out into the dish, and the mercury level in the tube dropped to about 30 inches (76 cm). But what was preventing it all from escaping?

Torricelli reasoned that the weight of the atmosphere (air) pressing on the surface of the mercury in the dish equaled the weight of the mercury left in the tube. The height of the mercury column is therefore a measure of air pressure. The whole device is known as a

The Magdeburg spheres were two hemispheres of copper. After the air had been pumped out, creating a vacuum, even 16 horses could not pull them apart.

barometer. Torricelli also noticed that the height of the column varied slightly from day to day depending on the weather, and deduced that atmospheric pressure must also vary daily. In 1647, French mathematician René Descartes (1596–1650) added a vertical scale to a Torricelli barometer, and used it to record weather observations. To this day, air pressure is one of the most important factors considered by weather forecasters. Pressure is still sometimes measured in inches or millimeters of mercury— "normal" pressure is 30 inches (760 mm).

Measuring atmospheric pressure

Atmospheric pressure also varies with altitude. The pressure at the top of a mountain is less than that at the foot of the mountain. (The pressure outside a high-flying jet plane is practically zero.) In 1771, over a century after Torricelli's death, Swiss geologist Jean Deluc (1727–1817) began using a sensitive barometer to measure the heights of mountains. A modern altimeter, used in airplanes, is also a modified barometer, although not the mercury type.

Torricelli's barometer was not very portable, even if Jean Deluc carried one up mountains. In 1797, a French scientist, Nicolas Fortin (1750–1831), invented a portable mercury barometer. The mercury reservoir was contained in a leather bag. By turning a screw, the bag could be squeezed slightly to bring the surface of the mercury in line with a level indicated by a pointer, and a vernier scale at the top of the tube allowed very accurate pressure readings to be taken.

Vacuum pumps

Returning to Torricelli's experiment, what was in the space above the mercury at the top of the closed tube? The short answer is "nothing." In fact, it was a vacuum, a space in which there is nothing at all. Scientists soon wanted to study vacuums and their effects, and

The Mercury Barometer

To recreate Torricelli's original experiment, the closed glass tube is first completely filled with mercury, and then placed upside down in the dish of mercury. The mercury column in the tube falls slightly, leaving a vacuum in the space above. Atmospheric pressure acting on the surface of the mercury in the dish holds up the mercury column. The height of the column above the surface measures the atmospheric pressure.

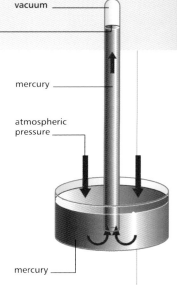

atmospheric pressure measured in inches/mm of mercury

vacuum

mercury

atmospheric pressure

mercury

needed a way to produce them in the laboratory. In 1654 physicist Otto von Guericke (1602–86), mayor of Magdeburg, Germany, invented the first air pump, so-called because it was designed to pump air out of a vessel. (Today we would call it a vacuum pump.) He used it to remove the air from between a pair of copper hemispheres, which became held tightly together by the force of atmospheric pressure. Even 16 horses could not pull them apart. Von Guericke's demonstration apparatus became known as the Magdeburg spheres.

Other, more efficient, vacuum pumps followed. In 1703, English physicist Francis Hawksbee (c.1666–1713) made a vacuum pump that Irish scientist Robert Boyle (1627–91) employed in his studies of air and other gases. German physicist Heinrich Geissler (1815–79) used his pump of 1855 to study electrical discharges at low pressures, and ten years later German-born British scientist Hermann Sprengel (1834–1906) mechanized Geissler's pump so that it could produce high vacuums. Still used today, it is a mercury vapor pump (or diffusion pump) in which the vapor "captures" molecules of air, and carries them away to produce a vacuum. It had very important applications in science, leading to the finding of the rare gases in air, the discovery of the electron, and the invention of the electric light bulb, among other things.

Curriculum Context

Students should understand that the impact of technological advances may be far-reaching.

Iron smelting

Iron has been known since ancient times, and the period from about 1100 B.C. is known as the Iron Age in the Middle East and Europe. But iron tools and weapons were rare, and reserved only for rich people until methods of smelting iron from its ores became widespread after the invention of the blast furnace in about 700 A.D.

Early metalworkers used simple blast furnaces to smelt iron. First they dug a hole in the ground, and built a chimney over it. They placed iron ore on top of smoldering charcoal in the pit. Using hand bellows, they forced air into the furnace, which raised the inside temperature, and produced molten iron.

The ancient Egyptians got their iron from meteorites picked up in the desert, and by about 1350 B.C. they had developed methods of welding it in a hot fire. At about the same time, the Hittites in Anatolia (modern Turkey) began using iron, and knowledge of ironworking spread to India and China. Ancient Greeks used iron bolts to join blocks of stone, and in about 400 B.C. Chinese craftsmen made statues from a type of cast iron that had a low melting point.

Early blast furnaces

The first blast furnace for iron, the Catalan forge in Spain, is thought to date from about 700 A.D. Another was constructed about a century later in Scandinavia. The principle involves simple chemistry, although, of course, that was unknown to the people of the time. The diagram left shows how it worked. The metalworkers made a furnace by digging a hole in the ground, and lining it with packed earth and charred reeds—a form of fine charcoal. They added a conical chimney made of clay and slag (impurities from a previous furnace).

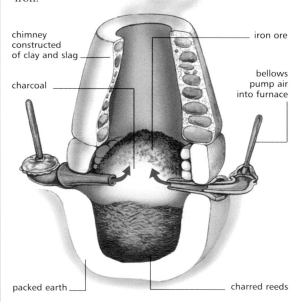

chimney constructed of clay and slag

charcoal

iron ore

bellows pump air into furnace

packed earth

charred reeds

An early woodcut showing workers smelting iron in a blast furnace.

The furnace was filled, or "charged," with a mixture of iron ore, limestone, and charcoal, and then it was set on fire. When it was hot, workers pumped bellows to force a blast of air through the furnace. The ore (iron oxide) changed into metallic iron by the action of carbon monoxide (CO), formed in turn by the action of the air on the charcoal (carbon). The main purpose of the limestone (calcium carbonate) was to form a slag with the silicate rock impurities in the ore. The slag floated on top of the molten iron. The molten iron itself could then be tapped through a hole near the bottom of the furnace.

Ore

A mineral or group of minerals from which a valuable constituent, especially a metal, can be profitably mined or extracted.

Blast furnaces, like the ones shown here at Coalbrookdale in England in 1830, helped to provide vital supplies of iron for the Industrial Revolution.

Curriculum Context

Students should be able to describe how changes in manufacturing technology affect business and industry.

Increasing efficiency

By the 14th century, England was Europe's main iron-producing country. Waterwheels powered the bellows to produce a continuous stream of air for the blast furnaces, which were able to produce up to 3.3 tons (3 tonnes) of iron a day. This output required large amounts of charcoal, produced by burning wood. As a result, most of Britain's forests were destroyed. Then in 1709 English iron founder Abraham Darby (c.1678–1717) began using coke (derived from coal) instead of charcoal. Darby's compatriot Dud Dudley (1599–1684) claimed to have previously used coal in a blast furnace, but that is unlikely because the sulfur in the coal would have spoiled the iron. Darby's development had a dramatic effect on the production and uses of cast iron, and cast-iron pans, pots, and kettles were soon common in every home in England.

Darby built his furnaces at Coalbrookdale on the banks of the Severn River. In 1742, his son Abraham Darby II

(1711–63) installed a steam engine to pump water from the river to power the bellows. His grandson Abraham Darby III (1750–91) took over the company in 1768, and built a lasting memorial to the family. In 1779, using prefabricated cast-iron sections, he completed an iron bridge over the Severn River at Coalbrookdale. It is 98 feet (30 m) long, and stands 39 feet (12 m) above the water. It still carries foot passengers, but it was closed to traffic in 1934.

The final improvements to the blast furnace came in the 1800s. In 1828, in Glasgow, Scotland, Scottish engineer James Neilson (1792–1865) improved its efficiency by preheating the air by sending it through a red-hot tube. The tube was heated at first by a coal fire and later by coal gas—a byproduct from coking furnaces. English inventor Edward Cowper (1819–93) improved Neilson's design in 1857 with his hot-blast stove, which used waste gases from the blast furnace itself to preheat the air.

Curriculum Context

The curriculum expects that students can research and describe the various contributions made by technologists and scientists.

Navigation at sea

The crew of a ship in the middle of an open ocean needs to know what direction the ship is traveling in and exactly where it is. A compass can indicate direction, and the magnetic compass was in regular use by the 1100s. But accurate positioning needs a knowledge of both latitude and longitude, which proved to be much more difficult to determine.

Polestar

The star Polaris, which lies nearly in a direct line with the axis of the Earth's rotation "above" the North Pole, making it apparently motionless from the Earth.

Latitude indicates an object's position in terms of its distance north or south of the equator. It is measured in degrees. For example, Philadelphia is at a latitude of 40° north. Latitude can be found by measuring the angle of a particular heavenly body above the horizon, and consulting books of tables or almanacs. At night the angle of the polestar or during the day the angle of the Sun at noon can be measured and compared with tables. Early sailors had various instruments for measuring these angles. Using a cross-staff, a sailor sighted along a 3-foot- (1-m-) long staff while moving a crosspiece until the lower end lined up with the horizon and the upper end coincided with the star or the Sun. The staff was calibrated in degrees from which the sailor could read off the angle. It was first described in about 1330 by French astronomer Levi ben Gershom (1288–1344), and used in Europe until the 18th century.

In 1594, English sailor John Davis (c.1550–1605) invented the backstaff. It was pointed in the opposite direction, and the operator did not need to look directly into the Sun. The quadrant was a similar instrument, used also by astronomers and by gunners to set the correct angles for aiming artillery pieces.

Curriculum Context

Students should be aware that technological changes often happen in small steps.

From octant to sextant

Then in 1731 English mathematician John Hadley (1682–1744) invented the octant—incorrectly named Hadley's quadrant at the time. The Anglo-American

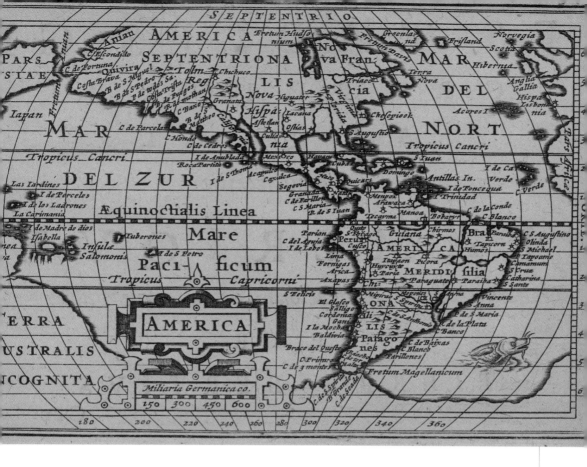

inventor Thomas Godfrey (1704–49) of Philadelphia then invented an almost identical instrument independently. In the octant a pivoted arm carries a mirror that can be moved to bring an image of the Sun in line with another mirror. The second mirror also gives a view of the horizon. The maximum angle it could measure was 45°. From there it was a simple step to the sextant (which measured up to 60°), introduced by Scottish naval officer John Campbell (c.1720–90) in 1757. The octant remained the standard navigational instrument for 250 years. It was even used on aircraft until it was finally supplanted by radio beacons, and the satellite-based GPS (global positioning system).

In 1884, an international conference agreed that the prime meridian (longitude 0°) should be the Greenwich meridian that runs through Greenwich

An early map of the New World showing lines of longitude and latitude.

finding Longitude

These diagrams show how to use a chronometer (a very accurate type of clock) to find a ship's longitude—its position east or west of the prime meridian at longitude 0°. The ship sails from Greenwich on the prime meridian at 12 noon local time. The chronometer is also set to 12 o'clock. After sailing west for five days, at 12 noon local time (easily gauged by using a sextant to plot the Sun's highest point) the chronometer reads 4 o'clock in the afternoon. In other words, local time is four hours behind Greenwich time, as shown by the chronometer. The Earth has rotated on its axis for four hours since it was 12 noon in Greenwich. The four hours represent 4/24, or 1/6, of a complete rotation, that is, 1/6 of 360,° or 60°. This ship's longitude is therefore 60° west.

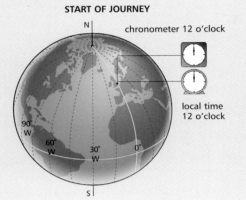

START OF JOURNEY

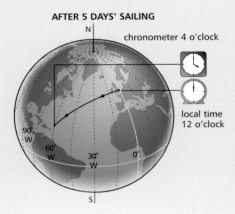

AFTER 5 DAYS' SAILING

Meridian

An imaginary arc on the Earth's surface from the North Pole to the South Pole that connects all locations with a given longitude.

Observatory in London. However, finding the longitude of any other place—its position east or west of the Greenwich meridian (longitude 0°)—proved to be far more difficult than calculating latitude. For centuries sailors measured the angle between the Moon and another heavenly body, and consulted tables called ephemerides that gave the day-to-day positions of the Moon. German astronomer Johann Müller (1436–76), also known as Regiomontanus, drew up the first tables in 1474. They were published in 1766 in the *Nautical Almanac* by English astronomer Nevil Maskelyne (1732–1811), and were subsequently revised every year.

The solution to the longitude problem lay in finding an accurate way of measuring time, which varies locally depending on longitude. For example, at 12 noon in London, England, it is 7.00 a.m. in Philadelphia (longitude about 75° west). So if we know the exact time at a given place when it is noon in London, we can calculate its longitude. To do this we need a chronometer, a very accurate clock. In 1714 the British government offered a prize of £20,000 to anyone who could produce such an instrument. A condition of the competition was that the "sea clock" had to gain or lose no more than 2 minutes after a six-week voyage to the West Indies and back.

Harrison's chronometer

English clockmaker John Harrison (1693–1776) took up the challenge, and in 1735 introduced his first chronometer. But it was his fourth instrument of 1759 that won the prize (or half of it, since the government retained the other half until Harrison could prove that the chronometer could be duplicated). Harrison did not receive the remainder until 1773, and then only after King George III pleaded Harrison's case.

index glass

rays from the Sun

rays from horizon

horizon glass

telescope

limb (graduated scale)

The Sextant

A navigator uses a sextant to measure the angle of the Sun (or at night a prominent star) above the horizon. Special tables convert the angle into the navigator's latitude, the angular distance north or south of the equator. The index glass (in fact, a mirror) reflects the Sun's rays onto a second mirror called the horizon glass. This reflects the rays along a telescope to the navigator's eye.

A shade glass cuts down the brightness and prevents eye damage. The navigator also looks through the plain (unsilvered) half of the horizon glass at the horizon, and adjusts the angle of the index glass until the Sun's image appears to be on the horizon. The graduated scale on the limb of the sextant then indicates the angle of the Sun above the horizon.

Benjamin Franklin

Benjamin Franklin was a complex character—an unusual combination of statesman and scientist. He played an important part in the development of the young United States, and made major discoveries in physics. He was also a talented inventor, and some of his inventions are still in use throughout the world today.

Benjamin Franklin was born in Boston. After leaving school, he was apprenticed to his older brother James, a printer. When 18, he took over publication of the *New England Courant*, a newspaper founded by his brother. Soon he went to Philadelphia to work as a printer himself. In 1724, he sailed for England. He returned home and published the first volume of *Poor Richard's Almanac* in 1733, a collection of articles to "convey instruction among the common people." He held various public offices, and helped draft the Declaration of Independence in 1766. He went to France to raise help for Americans in the War of Independence, and in Paris he saw the Montgolfier brothers' first hot-air balloon flight in 1783. He was a great supporter of the abolition of slavery. He retired from public life in 1788.

Scientific interests

Franklin also conducted scientific experiments. The best known involved attaching a metal key to the wet string of a kite, which he flew during a thunderstorm. Electric "fluid" flowing down the string caused sparks to jump between the key and a Leyden jar (a primitive electrical condenser). Franklin had established the electrical nature of lightning, and coined the words "positive" and "negative" to describe the two types of static electricity. Some scientists who tried to repeat the experiment were killed by lightning. Franklin, however, devised a means of protection: He invented the lightning rod, a pointed conductor fixed at the top of a building, and connected to the ground by a wire

Lightning

A discharge of atmospheric electricity, accompanied by a vivid flash of light, commonly from one cloud to another, sometimes from a cloud to the Earth.

Benjamin Franklin's best-known (but very dangerous) experiment, which he performed in 1752, involved flying a kite in a thunderstorm to study electricity. In 1824, the Franklin Institute was founded in Philadelphia in his honor.

attached to a plate in the soil. Today all tall buildings have lightning rods. He theorized that thunderclouds are electrically charged, and recognized the aurora borealis (northern lights) to be electrical in nature.

Franklin had many other scientific interests. He rejected Newton's corpuscular theory of light (that light travels as particles), favoring the wave theories of Robert Hooke and others. He suggested that the rapid heating of air near warm ground causes it to expand and spiral upward, producing tornadoes and waterspouts. He investigated the course of the Gulf Stream, the current of warm water that flows across the Atlantic Ocean, and he suggested that ships' captains should use a thermometer to locate and benefit from the current (or avoid it, depending on the direction they were sailing).

Curriculum Context

Students should know that historical perspective of scientific explanations demonstrates how scientific knowledge changes by evolving over time.

Locks and keys

Locks and keys have been used for thousands of years. They provided people with a secure way of protecting goods and premises from thieves and intruders as well as confining prisoners. Even some early locks were quite sophisticated.

One of the earliest known locks was found in the ruins of the palace of Khorsabad in Iraq. Made entirely of wood, this lock is probably 4,000 years old. The door is secured with a sliding wooden bolt. The lock mechanism, called a pin-tumbler, consists of several holes drilled through the bolt with matching pins attached to the door above. As the bolt is slid across the door, the pins drop into the holes, locking it in place. The key is a large wooden bar with a group of upright pegs that matches the pattern of holes. When the key is inserted, the pegs lift the pins out of the bolt, and the door is unlocked. Locks of this type are still used in parts of North Africa and the Middle East, and the falling pin design forms the basic principle of many locks, including the famous Yale-type lock.

Ancient Greek and Roman locks

The ancient Greeks were the first to use metal keys, but their locks were less sophisticated than the older pin-tumbler designs. The bolt was moved by an L-shaped key made from iron. The key was passed through a hole in the door and turned, engaging the bolt and drawing it back. This type of lock provided little security because it was not encoded in any way. Anyone who could fashion an L-shape of the right dimensions could open the door.

Roman locks were the first to be made entirely out of metal, usually iron for the lock and bronze for the key. The Romans invented wards, which are intricate patterns of matching slots on both key and lock.

Once the key is slotted onto the ward, it can be rotated around the ward rail to operate the bolt. Warded locks have always been relatively easy to pick, because special keys could be made to pass around the ward even if they did not fit perfectly.

An old wooden door in Umbria, Italy, with an attractive sliding bolt and lock mechanism.

Medieval locks

During the Middle Ages a great deal of skill was used in crafting locks, but the technology changed little. Keyholes were often hidden behind secret shutters to confuse the picker, and false keyholes were often cut in the door to waste would-be thieves' time. However, security still depended on complex warding. One innovation was the English 17th century letter-lock. A number of rings inscribed with letters or numbers were threaded onto a spindle. When the rings were turned to form a particular number or word, slots inside the rings were aligned, and the spindle could be drawn out.

Curriculum Context

The curriculum expects that students are able to research and describe the various major contributions of technologists and scientists.

Early modern locks

It was not until the 19th century that any real advances in lock design were made. In 1778 English locksmith Robert Barron patented a double-acting tumbler. A tumbler is a lever that falls into a slot, and cannot be moved unless it is raised to a set height. Inserting the key raises the tumblers, while turning it slides the bolt out. The Barron lock had two tumblers, and the key had

Padlocks

Padlocks are removable locks with a hinged or pivoting curved bar called a shackle, which can be used to join two objects together, most usually the two ends of a chain. The locking mechanism is enclosed in a steel case for protection. To shut the lock, the shackle is simply pushed into a hole in the steel case; inside, a lever falls into a slot at the tip of the shackle, holding it in place. A special combination or a key is then used to release the shackle and open the lock.

to raise each by a different amount before the bolt would slide. The principle behind this design is still used in all lever locks today, but a determined lock picker could still open Barron's lock.

In 1784 an entirely new lock was patented by English engineer Joseph Bramah (1748–1814). It used a very small key yet provided a level of security not achieved before. To manufacture his locks, Bramah constructed a geared lathe, one of the first metalworking machines designed for mass production. The locks were very expensive, but Bramah was so sure of their security that he offered a reward of £210—a huge sum in those days—to the first person who could pick one. This challenge stood for 67 years until a U.S. locksmith, A.C. Hobbs, succeeded and claimed the reward. However, picking the lock took Hobbs more than 50 hours!

By the middle of the 19th century the lock industry was booming. The fast-growing economies of the United States and Europe provided a huge demand for locks, and hundreds of new types of lock were patented. Most of these, however, were merely variations on existing lock designs.

Yale locks and time locks
The United States made its first and probably most lasting contribution to lock design in 1848. Linus Yale (1821–68) patented a pin-tumbler lock based on ancient principles. In the 1860s, he designed the Yale cylinder lock, with its familiar flat key and serrated edge. Pins are raised to the correct heights by the serrated edge, thus releasing the cylinder, which can then be turned. This type of lock is now widely used in the doors of cars and buildings.

In the 1870s a new crime wave swept across the United States; robbers would hold bank cashiers at gunpoint, and force them to open the safe. To combat this type of

Patent

A grant made by a government that confers upon the creator of an invention the sole right to make, use, and sell that invention for a set period of time.

Curriculum Context

Students should understand that science and technology are not separate from society, but rather part of society.

crime, U.S. inventor James Sargent built the first time lock in 1873. His lock contained a built-in clock, and could only be opened at a preset time.

Modern locks and keys

The importance of locks as a protection against thieves declined after World War II (1939–45), when the knowledge of explosives became widespread. Locks became more difficult to pick, and thieves usually ignored them and simply blasted them off.

Locks have been invented with many bizarre designs. Some resist explosives; others shoot, stab, or seize the hands of intruders. Other locks can be locked with one key, but only opened with another. The basic types remain the warded, lever, and pin-tumbler, although variations often combine the best features of each.

In buildings with many different locks, such as offices, schools, and prisons, it can be very useful to have a "skeleton key" that can open all the doors in the building. This master key can be shaped to avoid the warding of all the locks, or there may be two keyholes, one for the normal key, one for the master key. Alternatively, the locks can be fitted with two sets of tumblers and levers or, in the case of Yale locks, two concentric cylinders—one operating inside the other.

Today, locks are often computerized. The code is no longer physically encrypted on a key, but magnetically or digitally encoded on a card. Some locks can even recognize an individual's retina (the inner surface of the eye) or fingerprints. One of the ultimate locks, used on the U.S. nuclear missile launch system, can only be activated by two operators putting different keys into keyholes at opposite ends of the control console, and turning them at precisely the same time. One operator would be physically unable to reach far enough to turn both keys simultaneously.

Curriculum Context

Students should be aware that technological changes often happen in small steps.

Fingerprint

The distinctive ridges and patterns that appear on the ends of the fingers and thumbs, which are unique to each individual.

Types of Lock

A warded lock relies on a specific matching pattern of slots and grooves on both lock and key. Once inserted, the correct key can be slid onto the ward rail and rotated, drawing back the bolt (a bar, usually made from metal, that secures the door). Unfortunately, warded locks can be opened by keys that are shaped to avoid the wards rather than fitting perfectly.

key

ward rails

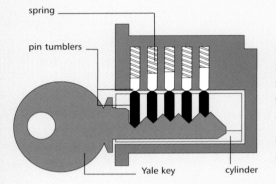

spring

pin tumblers

Yale key   cylinder

A Yale cylinder lock uses the ancient pin-tumbler principle. The pins themselves are cut into two separate parts of varying lengths. Notches cut into the flat key raise each pin to a specific height at which the cut between the two parts of the pin aligns with the edge of the cylinder. The cylinder can then be rotated, releasing the bolt.

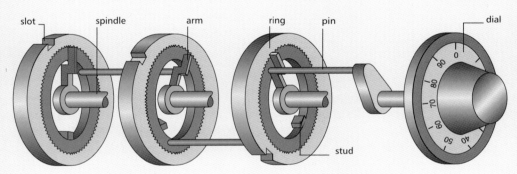

slot   spindle   arm   ring   pin   dial

stud

A combination lock consists of a series of rings threaded onto a central spindle. A slot is cut into the outer edge of each ring, and a raised stud is present on the inner surface. When the knob on the outside of the lock is rotated, the attached pin (in reality much shorter than shown) engages an arm on the spindle, which in turn engages the stud on the first ring. The rings are connected to one another by the same mechanism. By turning the knob through a specific series of clockwise and counterclockwise rotations, using the numbers etched onto the dial surface as a reference, the slots on the rings are aligned, allowing the bolt to be drawn out.

Balloons

For centuries people have looked skyward, casting an envious eye at the birds and dreaming of a day when they too could fly. The first attempts at flight used craft that could fly because they were lighter than the air itself—hot-air balloons, for example.

More than 2,000 years ago, Chinese children played with tiny hot-air balloons. They placed dry twigs inside empty eggshells and then set the twigs alight, heating the air inside the eggshells, and sending them flying upward. In the 1200s, the Mongols of Central Asia used a dragon-shaped hot-air balloon as a symbol to rally around. The first ascent of a hot-air balloon in the

The launch of the Montgolfier brothers' ornate hot-air balloon in November 1783. It carried two men on a 5.5-mile (9-km) journey over the city of Paris, France. Powered flight of heavier-than-air craft came much later, however.

Putting Balloons to Work

While both hot-air and hydrogen-filled balloons provided entertaining diversions from the routine of 18th-century life, they appeared at first to have no practical use. One man, however, soon realized that he could use tethered balloons to his advantage. French general Napoleon Bonaparte (1769–1821), who later became the emperor of France, formed the world's first ever military airborne division. Known as the Aérostiers, this intrepid group of tethered balloonists gave the French Army an advantage by revealing the exact location of an enemy's troops. For much of the following hundred years tethered balloons were used in this capacity by many different armies, including both sides during the American Civil War (1861–65).

Prussian soldiers on horseback chase a hot-air balloon used for spying on their positions.

Western world, however, did not occur until some 500 years later.

Understanding the science

Before that could take place, however, advances needed to be made in understanding the nature of gases, including the air. Through the work of such pioneers as Anglo-Irish chemist Robert Boyle (1627–91) people came to realize that different gases had different weights and that the gas contained inside a "bubble" would rise if it was lighter than the gas outside the bubble.

The Montgolfier brothers

On a sunny June day in 1783, French brothers Joseph-Michel Montgolfier (1740–1810) and Jacques-Étienne Montgolfier (1745–99) unveiled their new invention before a spell-bound audience in the marketplace in Annonay, southern France. The brothers burned straw and wood under a specially designed bag and thrilled onlookers, who watched open mouthed as the Western world's first hot-air balloon soared roughly 3,000 ft (900 m) into the air. In November of the same year, the Marquis d'Arlandes (1742–1809) and François Pilâtre de Rozier (1757–85) set about becoming the first people to take to the skies in another of the Montgolfier brothers' hot-air balloons.

In an age when television brings the wonders of the world into our homes on a daily basis, it is hard to imagine the effect that such a sight would have had on the crowd. Up until this point in history, as far as Westerners were concerned, flight was strictly for the birds. To the crowd in the marketplace the sight of that simple bag rising into the air would have been as awe inspiring as the first human footsteps on the Moon were to people nearly two hundred years later in the 20th century. When the balloon landed in a field on the outskirts of Paris, some peasant workers dropped to their knees in prayer, believing the two adventurers to be angels sent by God.

The first hydrogen balloon

Hot air was not the only gas being used to inflate balloons in 1783. The French physicist Jacques-Alexandre Charles (1746–1823) took to the air with his friend and colleague Frenchman Nicolas Robert just six months after the Montgolfier brothers first demonstrated their hot-air balloon.

Jacques-Alexandre Charles takes to the skies in his hydrogen-filled balloon during December 1783.

Using a balloon that had been filled with hydrogen (the lightest of all gases), the two men must have wondered what they had let themselves in for when their craft shot nearly one mile (1.5 km) up into the sky. Charles and Robert eventually returned safely to the ground and, against all the likely expectations, became ballooning enthusiasts.

The steam engine

From the time of the ancient Egyptians until the end of the 17th century, only wind and water power provided an alternative to the muscles of animals and humans. But the situation changed dramatically with the invention of the steam engine, which involved a sequence of events beginning in 1690, and finally culminating in 1765 with the work of James Watt.

It would be no exaggeration to say that engines drive the modern age. From airplanes and locomotives to power plants, rockets, and automobiles, all are driven by engines, which have developed from steam to nuclear power in little more than 200 years.

The word engine was once used to refer to almost any kind of machine, including a water mill. Strictly speaking, an engine that burns fuel to produce heat and some kind of useful motion is called a heat engine. The first engines heated water to produce steam; they were followed by engines that burned gasoline and diesel. Engines of the future may burn hydrogen or other "clean" fuels to help protect the environment.

First steam power

Although the first steam engines were not developed until the 18th century, experiments with steam as a form of power date back to Hero of Alexandria, a Greek inventor who lived around A.D. 60. His aeolipile was a ball filled with water that had two exhaust nozzles mounted on opposite sides. When the ball was heated, the water turned to steam, and emerged from the nozzles, causing the ball to spin around.

Boyle's gas laws

It was not until the 17th century that serious efforts were made to harness the power of steam. In 1660, the eminent English physicist and chemist Robert

Boyle (1627–91) devised a series of laws to describe the behavior of gases. These gas laws included the important observation that if a gas is heated up in a closed container, its pressure increases. This principle has been used in every engine made since then.

Cutaway view of the housing for a beam engine of the type that might have been used to pump water out of mines.

Atmospheric engines

The earliest steam engines did not use the pressure of steam to provide power. Instead, they used air pressure. For that reason they are more accurately called atmospheric engines. The first was devised by Denis Papin (1647–1712), a French physicist working in England. A vertical, open-ended cylinder with a close-fitting piston had water inside its base. A fire heated the base of the cylinder, causing the water to boil and turn into steam. Steam pressure lifted the piston, which

Newcomen's Atmospheric Engine

The Newcomen engine was the first genuine steam engine. Unlike Savery's engine, it used steam pressure to push the piston directly, not just atmospheric pressure. Even so, the engines were similar enough for Newcomen to do a deal with Savery so that he could market engines under Savery's patent.

Steam from a boiler forced a piston up an open-ended cylinder, and then cold water sprayed into the cylinder condensed the steam, creating a partial vacuum, which sucked the piston down again. The piston rod was connected to one end of a long beam; the other end of the beam was connected to a pump. As the piston went up and down, the beam rocked and worked the pump continuously.

A Newcomen engine could produce about 12 strokes a minute. But because it needed to heat the water and cool the steam at every stroke, it used a great deal of fuel. In 1765 Watt adapted Newcomen's engine by adding an external condenser. This improvement ensured that the cylinder stayed hot and the condenser remained cool all the time, saving large amounts of fuel.

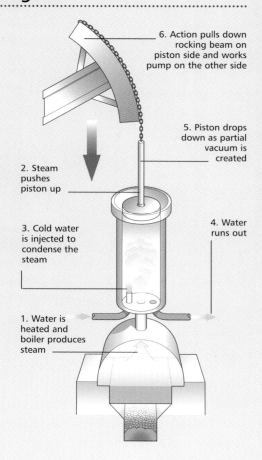

6. Action pulls down rocking beam on piston side and works pump on the other side

5. Piston drops down as partial vacuum is created

2. Steam pushes piston up

4. Water runs out

3. Cold water is injected to condense the steam

1. Water is heated and boiler produces steam

remained raised while the cylinder cooled. The steam condensed back to liquid water, creating a partial vacuum in the cylinder. Then atmospheric pressure on the upper end of the piston pushed it down again. A rope connected to the piston and moving over a pulley could be used to lift a load or work a pump.

A similar arrangement, patented in 1698 by English mining engineer Thomas Savery (c.1650–1715), made the atmospheric engine into a practical steam pump. It had no piston or other moving parts, just hand-operated valves to provide continuous operation. Steam from a boiler passed into a working chamber that was sprayed with cold water to condense the steam. The partial vacuum that was created as a result lifted water through a one-way valve into the chamber. Steam was then let in again, which forced the water out and up through another one-way valve.

Harnessing steam pressure

In 1712, English engineer Thomas Newcomen (1663–1729) perfected the first engine to use steam pressure to work a piston. Because of the way they were constructed, people generally referred to Newcomen's engines as beam engines. Newcomen could not patent his engine because its principle was too close to that of Thomas Savery's, so the two men went into partnership and built engines together.

This was the stage that steam power had reached in 1764, when Scottish engineer James Watt (1736–1819) received a model of a Newcomen engine to repair. He realized how much energy was wasted by first heating the cylinder and then cooling it. In 1765, he hit on the idea of adding a separate external condenser. In addition, he used steam to push up the piston and then—by admitting low-pressure steam on the other side—to push it down again. This double action greatly improved the efficiency of the machine.

Pressure

The force per unit area acting on an object, measured in units such as atmospheres, bars, or pascals.

Curriculum Context

Students should understand that scientists and engineers often work in teams.

James Watt's prototype steam engine of 1765. It was much more efficient than the earlier Newcomen steam engine.

Curriculum Context

The curriculum requires that students understand that technology often moves forward in small steps.

The next development was an increase in the pressure of steam in the engine—in the terminology of the day, "strong steam." However, this innovation had to await the introduction of improved cylinders with better-fitting pistons and boilers that were safe at high steam pressures. They became available by 1800, by the time Watt's master patent expired.

The following year English inventor Richard Trevithick (1771–1833) started building double-action, high-pressure engines. Trevithick removed the separate condenser, and used the waste steam to preheat the water entering the boiler. Within four years he built nearly 50 engines that were used mainly in mines in many parts of Britain, and eventually in Peru and other parts of South America.

By their very action, early steam engines produced an up-and-down motion. But most machines of the time, except pumps, required rotary motion. Until the advent of the steam engine most of them had been driven by waterwheels. Then in 1781 James Watt invented the "sun-and-planet" gear system to make his steam engines provide a rotary final drive.

Steam Engine

Steam from the engine's boiler enters the engine's cylinders through valves. The steam exerts pressure on the main piston, pushing it toward the end of the cylinder. This pulls the connecting rod toward the engine, and the crank (which links the connecting rod to the flywheel) converts the engine's reciprocating motion into the rotary motion of the flywheel. (The flywheel smooths the engine's power fluctuations by absorbing the engine's power and releasing it between strokes.) As the flywheel rotates, the cam-shaped eccentric strap also rotates, and the wide part of the eccentric strap pushes the eccentric rod to the left. The eccentric rod is linked to the smaller piston via the valve rod, and the piston is pushed to the end of the cylinder, switching the passage of steam into the main cylinder to the left-hand side. This puts pressure on the larger piston to move to the right, pushing the connecting rod, and still turning the flywheel clockwise. The eccentric strap rotates, pulling the smaller piston back to the right, starting the whole process again.

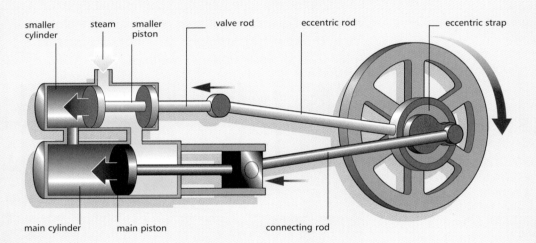

smaller cylinder | steam | smaller piston | valve rod | eccentric rod | eccentric strap

main cylinder | main piston | connecting rod

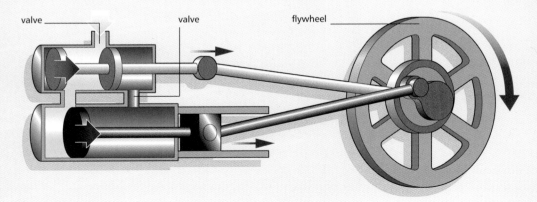

valve | valve | flywheel

Textile machines

The development of the mechanical spinning mule from the hand-operated spinning wheel took about six centuries. Yet within another 70 years, the Western textile industry became totally mechanized. Machines spun the yarn and wove lace, cloth, and carpets on power looms. Driven at first by water power and then by the new steam engines, textile machinery was at the forefront of the Industrial Revolution.

Industrial Revolution

The change to industrial methods of production that began in the late 18th century.

The first aid to spinning was the distaff, which consists of a long stick onto which wool is loosely wound. The spinner (or spinster), usually a woman, held the distaff under her arm, and teased out a continuous strand of wool, which she spun between the fingers of the other hand. The spun thread wound itself around a rotating spindle at its end. Historians have learned that the

ancient Mesopotamians used the distaff 7,500 years ago, and it competes with the wheel as the oldest-known invention.

The spinning wheel, which was in regular use in Europe from the 1200s, simplified the task by using a large vertical wheel. It had a belt drive to spin the spindle, while the spinner pulled a strand of wool from a vertical distaff. With her other hand she turned the wheel, although this task was mechanized by the addition of a foot treadle in the 16th century.

Improvements in spinning

Two major advances came in the 18th century. The English mechanic James Hargreaves (c.1720–78) invented the spinning jenny in 1764 (patented in 1770), and the spinning frame was invented by his compatriot Richard Arkwright (1732–92) in 1769.

Curriculum Context

Students should appreciate that engineers of high achievement are considered to be among the most valued contributors to their culture.

The spinning jenny allowed a worker to spin many strands of yarn at the same time. The machine was invented by English mechanic James Hargreaves in 1764.

The jenny was originally turned by hand, and mostly produced woolen yarn (eight threads at once on the first machines). The spinning frame was powered by a waterwheel, and made cotton yarn strong enough for the warp (lengthwise) threads in weaving. The two ideas were brought together in 1779 by the English weaver Samuel Crompton (1753–1827), who invented the spinning mule. It produced 48 strands of fine yarn at the same time. It is said to have been named "mule" because it is a hybrid of the two earlier machines.

In principle these two machines are much the same. The textile fibers, known as rovings, are wound onto rotating spindles that move on a frame. The frame first pulls the strands outward, twisting them to form yarn; it then moves back while the yarn is wound onto bobbins. After 1828, cotton was usually spun on the ring-spinning frame invented by the American John Thorpe (1784–1848). The rovings go through a set of high-speed rollers that draw them into fine threads. Each thread moves through a hole in a "traveler," which twists the thread as it winds it onto a rotating bobbin.

The Loom

A simple loom consists of a frame to hold sets of parallel warp threads. The weft (crosswise) thread is wound onto a shuttle, which the weaver works in and out of the warp (lengthwise) threads. Another frame called a heddle holds sets of vertical wires ending in rings through which the warp threads move. Controlled by treadles, the heddle lifts various sets of warp threads to create various different kinds of weave.

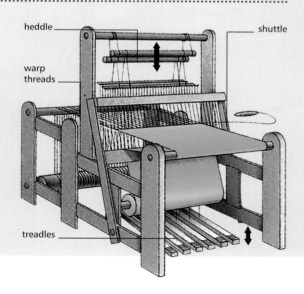

heddle

shuttle

warp threads

treadles

From yarn to cloth

Having produced the yarn, the weaver then has to make it into cloth. This is the function of the loom. At its simplest, the loom is a frame that holds a set of parallel threads called the warp. The weaver interweaves them at right angles with another thread—the weft—that is carried on a bobbin in a boat-shaped holder known as a shuttle. The first improvement was the addition of cords that pulled up every other warp thread to make it easier to pass the shuttle from side to side. Soon weavers added treadles to work the cords. Weaving sped up greatly in 1733 when English engineer John Kay (1704–c.1780) invented the flying shuttle, a mechanism that enables the weaver to "throw" the shuttle rapidly from side to side. Mechanized looms came next, driven by water power at first, but by steam engines after 1785, the year in which English inventor Edmund Cartwright (1743–1823) made the first steam-powered loom.

The interior of a linen manufacturer's weaving shed in the early days of mechanization, with rows of mechanically driven looms.

Farm machinery

After the invention of the plow and the sickle, which date from prehistoric times, there was little real progress in the technology of farming until the introduction of metal plowshares. Farmers in the Middle East used forged-iron plowshares in the 1900s B.C., but cast-iron plowshares did not appear in the West until toward the end of the 18th century.

Plow

An apparatus pulled by an ox, horse, or modern tractor, that is used to cut, lift, and turn soil in farm fields.

In 1785, English engineer Robert Ransome (1753–1830) invented a cast-iron plowshare. In the United States 12 years later Charles Newbold also patented a plow with a cast-iron plowshare. Still using horses to pull them, these plows could cut through the soil deeper and more easily than the wooden plows they replaced. A plow made completely of cast iron and therefore with replaceable parts was first made in 1819 by American engineers Stephen McCormick (1784–1875) and, independently, Jethro Wood (1774–1834). These plows were produced in quantity in 1839 by the American industrialist John Deere (1804–86).

By 1862, Dutch farmers were using steam plows. They had reversible plowshares mounted in a wheeled frame that was winched from one side of a field to the other by a pair of steam traction engines. Other farmers in Europe and the United States used steam tractors to pull standard plows.

Mechanization of sewing and reaping

After the farmer had plowed the land and harrowed (cultivated) the soil, the next step was to plant the seed. Since ancient times the way to do this had been to broadcast, or scatter, the seed by hand. A technological breakthrough had come earlier with the invention of the mechanical seed drill in 1701 by English agriculturist Jethro Tull (1674–1741). Using this machine, the farmer sowed the seed in parallel rows,

A farming scene in the 18th century. Horses provide the power for plowing and wind provides the power for grinding corn.

making the crop easier to weed by hoeing and easier to harvest. After harvesting, crops such as wheat had to be threshed to remove the grain. This too was a labor-intensive operation using whiplike flails until Scottish millwright Andrew Meikle (1719–1811) invented the threshing machine in 1786.

The last major farming process to be mechanized was reaping. Credit for the key invention usually goes to Cyrus McCormick (1809–84), whose father Robert had also tried but failed to build such a machine. Cyrus made his first reaper in 1831, when he was only 22 years old, and patented a machine in 1834. He did not exploit it for three years, but then started manufacturing reapers on a large scale. By 1859,

Reaper

Any farm machine that cuts cereal crops in the field.

Curriculum Context

The curriculum requires that students are able to describe how changes in technology affect business and industry.

he formed a partnership with his brother Leander. In 1879, they created the McCormick Harvesting Machine Company, which owned a large factory in Chicago that made 4,000 machines every year.

In 1827, before Cyrus McCormick patented his machine, Scottish clergyman Patrick Bell (1799–1869) had made a different reaper. He sent four examples of his machines to the United States, and may have stimulated McCormick in his endeavors. And in 1833 American engineer Obed Hussey (1792–1860) invented yet another type of reaper. His improved machine of 1847 was better than McCormick's for reaping grass and making hay, but Hussey did not have McCormick's organizational and business sense. McCormick reapers were prominently displayed in 1851 at the Great Exhibition in London and at the Paris International Exposition of 1855.

Teams of horses and their agricultural equipment in Manitoba, Canada, demonstrate the reliance on horse power in the days before tractors.

Combine harvesters and tractors

Also in the 1830s, following the pioneering work of American inventor John Lane, various engineers began to make combine harvesters. These machines not only cut the wheat, they also bundled it into sheaves. Separate binding machines were invented, notably by American John Appleby (1840–1917) in 1878. Later combines also threshed the grain, but the heavy machines needed ten or more horses to pull them.

The invention of the steam traction engine and later, in 1908, of the steam caterpillar tractor, overcame this disadvantage. Two years later gasoline-driven combine harvesters began to take over. At first a separate tractor pulled the harvester, as with the Allis-Chalmers Company's "All-Crop Harvester" of 1935. Later, motive power was built into the machine, and self-propelled combines became a common sight on the prairies.

Curriculum Context

Students should understand that some technological solutions can have both intended benefits and unintended consequences.

Canal transportation

The main method of moving heavy goods before the coming of the railroads was by canal. By the end of the 18th century timber, coal, and iron ore—all the raw materials needed for the emerging Industrial Revolution—as well as finished goods were towed on barges along the canals, with horses as the motive power.

The first canals for transportation were built by Chinese engineers more than 2,000 years ago. Extensive canal systems were used for drainage and irrigation in northern India and by the Middle Ages in the

Netherlands. Canals for industrial transportation were first used in England in 1757 after the engineer Henry Berry (1720–1812) completed the Sankey Brook Navigation near St. Helens in the north of England. The canal at St. Helens included a pair of side-by-side locks known as staircase locks.

The first canal of economic importance was the Bridgewater Canal near Manchester, England. It was designed by engineer James Brindley (1716–72), and completed in 1761. At its narrowest it was 26 feet (8 m) wide, and was a contour (gravity-flow) canal with no locks. A canal that takes a more direct route needs

Curriculum Context

The curriculum requires that students can describe the technological systems used in transportation.

An early print of a canal aqueduct (a bridge that carries a water course over a valley) in Devon, England.

locks for coping with inclines, tunnels for going through hills, and aqueducts for crossing valleys.

Boats for canals

On Brindley's later canals the locks were just over 13 feet (4 m) wide. The barges using these canals thus had to be narrower than that, but they could be up to 72 feet (22 m) long—the maximum length of a lock. As a result, they were called narrowboats. They could carry a load of 33 tons (30 tonnes), while a wagon could carry just 2.2 tons (2 tonnes), and a packhorse's load could not usually exceed 300 pounds (135 kg).

Other canals soon followed. In 1773 the British government commissioned Scottish engineer James Watt (1736–1819) to survey a route in Scotland that would link a series of lochs (freshwater lakes) in order to join the North Sea and the North Atlantic Ocean. Site engineer Thomas Telford (1757–1834), a fellow Scot, began work in 1803, and the first vessel sailed through the canal in 1822. The first canal to take seagoing ships was completed in England in 1819 to connect the southwest town of Exeter with the sea.

North American canals

In North America, the first canal fitted with locks was probably the short waterway at Coteau-du-Lac, Quebec, built in 1779 by English engineer William Twiss (1745–1827) to bypass a stretch of rough water on the St. Lawrence River. In 1825, the Erie Canal was

Curriculum Context

Students should be able to analyze and discuss human influences on an aquatic environment, including transportation.

Traveling by canal was an alternative to riding in a coach or on horseback, but a horse still provided the motive power.

The Lock

Key to the development of canals is the pound, or chamber, lock. It effectively encloses a stretch of water so that it can be gradually raised or lowered. Invented in ancient China, locks were perfected in Holland and Italy in about 1370.

A canal lock has a pair of hinged gates at each end. They close at an angle that faces upstream (so that the pressure of down-flowing water helps keep them shut). Sluices in or around the gates can be raised or lowered to let water in and out of the lock. Consider a boat approaching a closed

lock from upstream. Here is the sequence of actions:

Open the sluices in the upstream gates until the lock is full of water. 1. Open the upstream gates and allow the boat to enter the lock. 2. Close the gates behind it. Open the sluices in the downstream gates until the water level falls to that of the water on the downstream side of the gates. 3. Open the downstream gates, and allow the boat to exit the lock. For a boat traveling in the opposite direction the sequence is reversed.

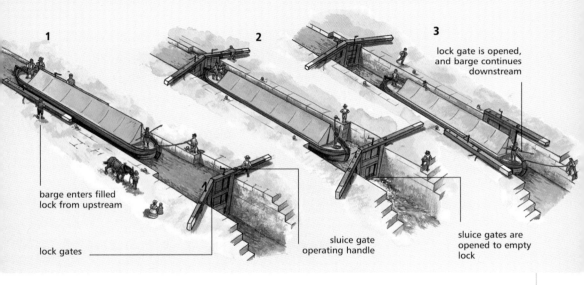

1

barge enters filled lock from upstream

lock gates

2

sluice gate operating handle

3

lock gate is opened, and barge continues downstream

sluice gates are opened to empty lock

completed to carry grain from the Great Lakes to New York City via the Hudson River. The 362-mile (583-km) canal was 39 feet (12 m) wide and 4 feet (1.2 m) deep, and needed 83 locks to cross the high ground west of Troy. In less than ten years receipts from tolls more than repaid the $7 million spent on its construction. The enlarged modern canal, now part of the New York State canal system, can carry barges displacing up to 2,204 tons (2,000 tonnes).

The beginnings of railroads

Railroads have their origins in the 16th century, when miners in various European countries used horses to pull wagons along wooden "roads" consisting of beams of timber laid lengthwise along the ground. But when the much heavier steam locomotives replaced horses, stronger and more rigid iron rails replaced timber balks, and the "iron road" was born.

As early as 1556 German scientist Georgius Agricola (1494–1555) described a mining railway that ran on wooden poles. In the coal mines of the English Midlands at the end of the 17th century horses pulled the empty trucks up the inclines to the mines, and then

Crowds gather to watch George Stephenson drive *Locomotion* at the opening of the Stockton & Darlington Railway in 1825. On opening day the passengers had to ride in open coal trucks.

the loaded trucks took themselves down again under the force of gravity. When industrialist Abraham Darby (c.1678–1717) began making cheap cast iron in the early 1700s, stronger cast-iron rails became available.

The first steam locomotive was built in 1803 by English engineer Richard Trevithick (1771–1833). He ran it along 10 miles (16 km) of cast-iron track from the Pen-y-Darren Ironworks to the Glamorganshire Canal in South Wales. The locomotive and rolling stock had smooth, unflanged wheels, and there was a lip on the outer edge of the track. Four years later Trevithick built a circular track in Euston, London, and charged people a shilling to chase their tails on his train—which was called *Catch Me Who Can.*

Cast iron

A hard, brittle form of iron that contains 2 to 4.5 percent carbon, which makes it very fluid when molten and easier to cast into complex shapes.

Curriculum Context

Students should understand that in the past two centuries, Europe has contributed significantly to the industrialization of Western and non-Western cultures.

The growth of commercial railroads

The first railroad to carry passengers regularly as well as freight opened in 1825. With locomotives built by English engineer George Stephenson (1781–1848), the Stockton & Darlington Railway ran for 26 miles (42 km); but until 1833 passengers traveled in horse-drawn coaches, and only freight was steam hauled. The first inter-city line, the Liverpool & Manchester Railway, opened in 1830, and the first train was hauled by Stephenson's *Rocket*. Built mainly to carry cotton from the port of Liverpool to the mills in Manchester in the northwest of England, the line had to cross an extensive bog. Stephenson (who was also the railroad's chief construction engineer) overcame the problem by building it on compacted hurdles "floating" on the waterlogged ground.

Railroads also sprang up in other countries. The year 1830 saw the inauguration of the Baltimore & Ohio Railroad, which initially ran for 13 miles (21 km) from Baltimore to Ellicott's Mills. To operate it, American engineer Peter Cooper (1791–1883) built *Tom Thumb*, the first locomotive to be made in the United States. The Philadelphia & Columbia Railroad opened with horse-drawn vehicles in 1831, but within three years it had steam locomotives. The longest railroad in the world at the time, the South Carolina Railroad, also started operations in 1831. It ran for 154 miles (248 km) from Charleston to Hamburg.

In 1832, the first steam-hauled line in France opened between St. Étienne and Lyons; and in 1835 Germany's first railroad opened between Nürnberg and Fürth with a locomotive called *Der Adler* (*The Eagle*), built by English engineer Robert Stephenson (1803–59). By 1840, there were also railroads in Austria, Ireland, and the Netherlands. As the new railroads appeared, moving goods by slower, water-born barges became uneconomic, and canals fell into disrepair.

Curriculum Context

Students should be able to describe the differences between the various transportation modes.

Rails, switches, and signals

As well as locomotives and rolling stock, railroads need other equipment. The "road" of the original railroads employed iron rails. They were made of cast iron, at first with a right-angled section to keep the wheels on the track. Soon these flanged rails were replaced. The flanges were put on the wheels of the vehicles, which ran on short "fish-bellied" rails that were straight on top but curved beneath to make them thicker (and stronger) in the center. But cast-iron rails often broke. From 1858, they were replaced by steel rails, introduced by English steelmaker Henry Bessemer (1813–98).

To enter sidings and branch lines, railroads need switches (known as "points" in Europe). They were invented as early as 1789 by English engineer William Jessop (1745–1814) for primitive tramway systems. As soon as trains started running into each other, signals were invented. They took the form of disks or arms that rotated or pivoted like semaphore signals. In 1849, the New York and Erie Company introduced block signaling, which does not allow a train to enter a section of track until the previous train has left it. Soon block signals were linked electrically.

Laborers replacing railroad tracks. Sections of track are heavy, and this was arduous work.

Steel

A generally hard, strong, durable, malleable alloy of iron and carbon, usually containing between 0.2 and 1.5 percent carbon, often with other constituents.

Evidence of fossils

Fossils are the remains of plants and animals that have been dead for a very long time. Most are the hard parts of animals—bones, teeth, or shells—that have been changed to rock. Some, such as the outlines of plants in coal or sedimentary rocks, are impressions. Even footprints can form fossils, leaving evidence of where creatures walked through soft mud millions of years ago.

Curriculum Context

Students should understand that fossils provide evidence about the plants and animals that lived long ago.

Curriculum Context

Students should know that fossils indicate that many organisms, which lived long ago are extinct.

In 1517, the Italian physician and poet Girolamo Fracastoro (*c.*1478–1553) was probably the first person to suggest that fossils are the remains of once-living organisms. But no one took much notice at the time, and it was not until the fossil finds in Europe of the late 18th century that scientists began to realize that fossils can tell us a great deal about the history of living things and the rocks in which they are found.

In 1793, French naturalist Jean-Baptiste Lamarck (1744–1829) revived the idea that fossils represent ancient organisms, and this time other scientists began to listen. Two years later his compatriot Georges Cuvier (1769–1832) discovered one of the first dinosaur fossils, although the word "dinosaur," which comes from Greek words meaning "terrible lizard," was not coined until 1842 by English fossil-hunter Richard Owen (1804–92).

Fossil formation

Paleontologists (the name for scientists who study fossils) recognized several ways in which fossils can form. One requirement is for the animal remains to be quickly buried before the carcass can decompose or be eaten by scavengers. The best place for that to happen is under water in the mud or sediment at the bottom of a lake or sea. That is also the place where sedimentary rocks form. Remains embedded in sediment may be dissolved by water, leaving behind a perfect mold. Minerals may be deposited in the mold, forming a

A fossil ammonite. Ammonites evolved around 400 million years ago before dying out 65 million years ago. They are often called index fossils, because it is possible to link the rocks in which they are found to specific geological time periods.

cast often made from a totally different type of rock than the sediment. Footprints or animal tracks in mud can be preserved in a similar way. Whole animals are preserved only occasionally, as with insects trapped in amber (fossilized tree resin) or mammoths buried in the frozen ground of the permafrost. The tar pits at Rancho La Brea in California have also preserved complete prehistoric skeletons.

Discovering fossils

Sedimentary rocks often make up the structure of sea cliffs. As the cliffs become eroded by waves and weather, they release any fossils they contain. The fossils can be seen sticking out of a cliff or lying on the beach below. In 1811 English schoolgirl Mary Anning (1799–1847) chose just such a location to take a walk. On a beach in Dorset, southern England, she came across a complete fossil skeleton of an ichthyosaur, a fishlike reptile that swam in the seas 150 million years ago during the Mesozoic Era. The 12-year-old sold her find to a local museum and then went on to become one of the world's best-known fossil collectors.

The ages of rocks

Over millions of years, layers of deposits form strata of sedimentary rocks one above the other. As long as no great Earth movements disturb the order, the younger rock layers are always found on top of older ones. In 1816 English geologist William Smith (1769–1839) pointed out that the age of a fossil must be the same as the rock in which it is found. It also works the other way: A rock with a fossil in it must be the same age as that fossil. This correlation provided a new method of geological dating. Of course, it could not provide the absolute age of either; that required later methods such as dating rocks or fossils by their radioactivity.

This reconstruction shows a sequence of fossil formation, and demonstrates how the hard parts of animals, such as shells, bones, and teeth, become converted into rock over many thousands of years.

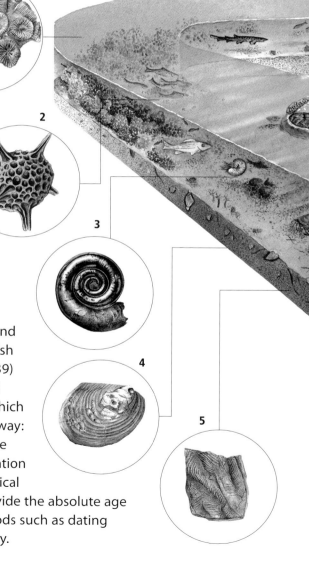

1. Coral skeletons (form reefs)
2. Silica skeleton of zooplankton
3. Ammonite shell
4. Bivalve (mollusk) shell
5. Trace fossils of tracks in mud
6. Graptolite (planktonlike) fossils

7. Petrified wood from tree
8. Carbonized leaves
9. Insect trapped in amber

Electricity

Of all the inventions associated with power and energy, electricity has probably been the one that has changed society the most. Electricity drives machines everywhere. Moreover, it also allows machines and their power source to be separated by vast distances.

If the people of ancient civilizations traveled forward in time, there is one modern invention in particular that would seem like magic to them—electricity. Who could have dreamed of simply flicking on a switch to light a room, boil water, or drive a locomotive?

Forms of electricity

We are most familiar with electricity in the form of electric currents, which pump around circuits driving televisions, PCs, and stoves. But the pioneers knew only static electricity, the form that causes lightning, and the sudden shocks built up from walking on carpets. The grandfather of static electricity was probably Greek philosopher Thales of Miletus (c.624–546 B.C.), who discovered in the sixth century B.C. that if he rubbed a type of fossilized tree resin called amber, it would attract light objects such as straw and feathers. The Greek word for amber is *elektron*, which gives us our words electricity and electron (the subatomic particle that carries electricity).

It was not until the 17th century that static electricity, or electrostatics, came to be understood. Around 1600 English physicist and doctor William Gilbert (1544–1603) suggested electricity was caused by a fluid called humor, which could be removed from a piece of amber when it was rubbed. In 1733, French chemist Charles du Fay (1698–1739) showed that electric charges came in two varieties: "vitreous," which we would call a positive charge today; and "resinous," which we would call a negative charge.

Curriculum Context

The curriculum requires an understanding of the concepts of electricity and magnetism.

Static electricity

An accumulation of electric charge on an insulated body.

Currents and their effects

Although the ancient Greeks knew about the phenomenon of static electricity, it was not until 2,000 years later that current electricity was discovered. In 1780, an Italian professor of anatomy, Luigi Galvani (1737–98), found that an electric charge made the muscles of a dead frog's leg contract, causing the leg to twitch, and he concluded this was caused by something inside the muscle. Alessandro Volta (1745–1827), professor of natural philosophy at a nearby university, believed that the effect was caused by the flow of electricity around a circuit. Between them they had discovered electric current. Volta found he could produce electric currents with a device made up of alternate layers of silver or copper, card or dried wood pulp that had been soaked in salt water, and zinc. He had produced the world's first battery, which became known as a Voltaic pile after its inventor.

A battery uses a chemical reaction to produce an electric current, but an electric current can also be used to produce a chemical reaction, in a process called electrolysis. Several British scientists, including

Curriculum Context

The curriculum requires that students can research and describe the historical development of the concepts of electrical and magnetic force.

German physicist and engineer Otto von Guericke (1602–86) made a primitive electric generator consisting of a globe of sulfur that built up a large charge when it was rubbed.

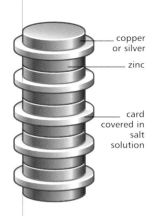

copper
or silver

zinc

card
covered in
salt
solution

The structure of a
Voltaic pile. The
device, the first
battery, produced
an electric current.

Curriculum Context

Students should be able to
demonstrate that electricity
can flow in a circuit and can
produce heat, light, sound,
and magnetic effects.

chemist Sir Humphry Davy (1778–1829), pioneered this useful science, called electrochemistry. It gave rise to electroplating, in which one metal can be coated with a layer of a different metal using electrolysis.

During the first half of the 19th century scientists around the world devoted themselves to conquering the mysteries of electricity using the new batteries to power their experiments. German physicist Georg Simon Ohm (1789–1854) showed that when different materials conduct electricity, the amount of resistance they offer to the passage of a current depends on their size, and the material from which they are made. The eminent British physicist James Joule (1818–89) demonstrated how a particular quantity of electric current could be used to produce an equivalent amount of heat—a property now used in all kinds of electric appliances from toasters to irons and stoves.

Electricity and magnetism

Perhaps most important was the research that showed electricity and magnetism were two sides of the same thing. In 1820, Hans Christian Ørsted (1777–1851), a professor of physics in Denmark, showed that an electric current flowing through a wire would deflect a nearby compass needle. This demonstrated that an electric current could produce magnetism. French mathematician and physicist André-Marie Ampère (1775–1836) worked out the mathematical theory behind Ørsted's findings. Electric current is now measured in amperes, or amps, in honor of Ampère.

If electricity could produce magnetism, could magnetism produce electricity? This was confirmed separately by British physicist and chemist Michael Faraday (1791–1867) and U.S. physicist Joseph Henry (1797–1878) between 1820 and 1831. These findings were combined in a theory of electromagnetism by British physicist James Clerk Maxwell (1831–79).

Static and Current Electricity

Electrons are tiny, negatively charged particles that, along with protons and neutrons, make up atoms. They can also exist independently, and are responsible for most of the phenomena that we know as electricity.

Static electricity is caused by a buildup of electric charge. If you walk on a carpet, friction between your shoes and the fibers causes electrons to move from your body to the carpet. This makes you positively charged. The more you walk, the bigger the charge you build up. Eventually, when you touch a metal object, the charge flows rapidly back to ground and can give you an electric shock. Lightning occurs in much the same way when clouds pass through the air. The Van de Graaff generator, invented by U.S. physicist Robert Van de Graaff (1901–67), is a machine that can produce over a million volts of static electricity for use in particle physics experiments. Friction caused by a comb at the base of the machine loads an upward-moving conveyer belt with positive charges that accumulate in the hollow, metal sphere at the top.

If static electricity is caused by a buildup of electrons in one place, current electricity is caused when the electrons flow around a closed path called a circuit. A lightning bolt is a crude type of circuit between a cloud and the Earth. The bulb, battery, and switch in a flashlight form a simple but effective circuit. When the switch is in the "off" position, the circuit is broken, and the bulb does not light up; when the switch is in the "on" position, the power is supplied by the battery and travels to the bulb, which lights up.

VAN DE GRAAFF GENERATOR

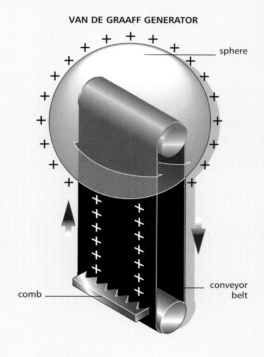

sphere

conveyor belt

comb

FLASHLIGHT CIRCUIT

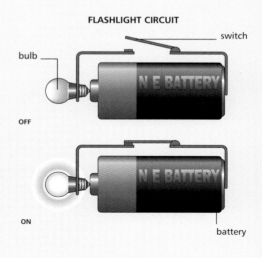

switch

bulb

N E BATTERY

OFF

N E BATTERY

ON

battery

Michael Faraday in his laboratory. He played a major part in developing our understanding of electromagnetism. He also discovered the laws of electrolysis and produced early types of electric motor, dynamo, and transformer.

Curriculum Context

The curriculum requires that students understand that electricity and magnetism are two aspects of a single electromagnetic force.

Electric engines and the generation of power

Until the start of the 19th century electricity had little practical use. But the principles of electromagnetism changed that. In the 1820s, Joseph Henry in the United States, and British electrical engineer William Sturgeon (1783–1850), produced working electromagnets (temporary magnets produced by electric currents). By 1832 Sturgeon had produced a practical electric motor by making a coil of wire rotate in the magnetic field created by large, permanent magnets. Sturgeon then invented a device called a commutator, which reverses the electric current every half-turn of the motor and so keeps it rotating in the same direction. This invention has been used in most electric motors ever since.

A similar electromagnetic engine was patented in the United States in 1837 by blacksmith-turned-inventor Thomas Davenport (1802–51) and later developed by U.S. inventor W.H. Taylor. Taylor's machine looked like a small wooden water wheel mounted on trestles. Seven coils of iron were fastened to the wheel, and four electromagnets attached to the frame. The wheel rotated when the current was switched on. The first commercial electric motors were built in 1873 by Belgian engineer Zénobe T. Gramme (1826–1901), who was using electric motors in his factory the next year.

Just as electricity can produce magnetic effects and rotate an electric motor, so magnetism can generate electricity. Generators were developed from Michael Faraday's research from the 1830s onward. Originally called magneto-electric machines, they were developed on a commercial scale by Gramme from 1870 onward. Gramme was the first person to produce a continuous current from a reliable machine.

The development of the arc light in the 1840s and filament lamps in 1879 led to an enormous interest in generating electric power on a large scale. The production of electric motors and heating filaments, and their use in a range of appliances confirmed that the age of electricity was at hand. All that remained was to generate electric power reliably on a large scale, and find a way of transmitting it to wherever it was needed. Perhaps the best-known early experiments were the steam-powered plants built at Holborn Viaduct in London, and at Pearl Street in New York. Both of these were built in 1882 by U.S. inventor and lighting pioneer Thomas Edison (1847–1931).

Magnetic Fields

Surrounding every magnet there is a field of force known as a magnetic field. Faraday carried out experiments to study the interaction and interrelationships between such fields and electric currents flowing in wires and other conductors. This is the branch of physics we now call electromagnetism. It is the basis of most electrical machines from motors and dynamos to the electric bell, the relay, and the solenoid (a type of electric switch).

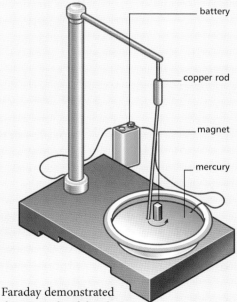

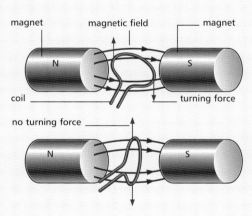

When a current is passed through a coil in a magnetic field, the field flows in opposite directions on the two sides of the coil, creating a turning force. When the coil has rotated until it is at right angles to the field lines, there is no turning force.

Faraday demonstrated the principle of the electric motor with this simple apparatus. A copper rod, pivoted at the top, dips into a pool of mercury alongside a vertical magnet. When a current flows along the rod, the rod rotates around the magnet.

The revolver

The first pistols—the original "handguns"—were made in the 1400s. They were muzzle-loading weapons that fired a lead ball or bullet using black powder (gunpowder) as the propellant charge. The means of igniting the charge improved over time from the original matchlock through the wheel lock, snaphaunce, flintlock, and percussion cap to the modern-day cartridge.

Flintlock

A mechanism that ignites the charge in a muzzle-loading pistol or musket.

Most of the early pistols had one thing in common: They could fire only one shot. There were a few double-barreled flintlocks, but the most effective way of firing more than one shot was to carry more than one loaded pistol. One attempt at increasing the number of shots available was the invention of the pepperbox pistol, which had several barrels. They were rotated in turn by hand to bring a new loaded barrel in front of the firing mechanism each time. But these weapons were relatively heavy and difficult to aim accurately.

The revolver

Another solution is the revolving pistol, or revolver, which has a cylinder bored with a number of loaded chambers that can be fired in turn as they align with a single barrel. There are examples of flintlock revolvers (in which the spark from a flint ignites the charge), but the revolver only came into its own when the percussion cap became the means of ignition after 1807. In this type of weapon each chamber in the cylinder leads to a narrow hole ending on the outside with a nipple holding a percussion cap. When the pistol is fired, the hammer falls on the cap, which explodes and fires the charge. The chambers are loaded from the front, so it is still a muzzle-loading weapon.

Curriculum Context

Students should be able to describe how the development and use of technology is influenced by past events.

The first percussion revolvers were made in England after about 1820 by an American gunsmith, Elisha Collier of Boston. He based the design on an earlier

A selection of handguns, or pistols, ranging from single-shot pocket pistols (left) to multiple-shot revolvers.

flintlock pistol that had been patented in the United States by Artemus Wheeler (1785–1850) in 1818. Within a few years many gunsmiths in a number of countries were producing percussion revolvers. But the first manufacturer to make reliable revolvers in quantity was the American Samuel Colt (1814–62), who obtained his first patent in England in 1835 (and subsequently in the United States in 1836).

The original Colts were single-action guns, meaning that the shooter had to cock the hammer by hand (a movement that also rotates the cylinder), and then pull the trigger to fire the pistol. In 1851 a rival gunsmith, Englishman Robert Adams, made the first of a series of double-action revolvers: One pull of the trigger rotates the cylinder, cocks the gun, and then fires it. Obviously it can be fired faster than a single-action weapon. The Beaumont–Adams revolver of 1855 (designed by Adams and Frederick Beaumont, a lieutenant in the British army) offered a choice of either single action or double action.

Beaumont-Adams revolvers favored

At first Colt sold his revolvers to the British army and navy, and he built a factory in London to produce the weapons. In general it was only the officers who carried pistols, but they favored the Beaumont–Adams revolvers. Although the Colts were more accurate over long distances, the Beaumont–Adams revolvers were quicker to fire, and their larger caliber (bore diameter) gave them greater "stopping power" (the ability to maim or kill an enemy). These were both crucial factors in hand-to-hand fighting. Colt closed his armory in London, although he continued to manufacture arms in his home town of Hartford, Connecticut, and to sell them throughout the world.

Cartridges

By about 1850, metal-cased cartridges were becoming available—at first for rifles. In the United States, Horace Smith (1808–93) and Daniel Wesson (1825–1906) designed a rim-fire cartridge, so-called because the percussion cap that fires it is located in the rim of the base of the cartridge case. A cylinder to take such a cartridge has to be bored all the way through, unlike the chambers of muzzle-loading weapons. American gunsmith Rollin White patented such a system in 1855. His pistol was a failure, but he held the patent rights to the cylinder needed by Smith and Wesson, and they had to pay a license fee to use it. The first Smith and Wesson cartridge revolvers went on sale in 1857.

When the Rollin White patent expired in 1869, other manufacturers soon produced cartridge weapons. John Adams (brother of Robert) developed a double-action cartridge revolver in 1867. But one of the most famous was the single-action Colt Peacemaker of 1873, which remained in production until the early 1940s.

Anatomy of a Revolver

Samuel Colt was successful in his business of producing handguns not only because they were well designed, but also because all the component parts were standardized. In this way thousands could be manufactured and assembled easily on a production line.

The central part of a revolver—which is short for revolving pistol—is the cylinder. As its name suggests, it is a cylinder of metal bored through with a number of chambers that hold the cartridges. Samuel Colt's early revolvers were single-action revolvers. The operator had to pull the hammer back manually against a spring to cock it. This action rotated the chamber and brought a cartridge in line with the barrel and the firing pin. When the trigger was squeezed, the spring was released, and the hammer and firing

pin were forced against the percussion cap at the base of the cartridge.

Later model Colts were double-action revolvers. In these weapons the hammer was cocked and then released to fire the cartridge in one single trigger movement, making rapid firing much easier.

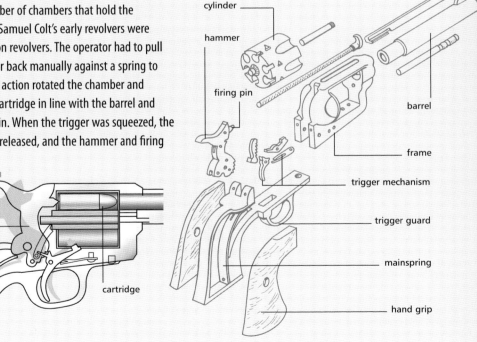

fore sight

cylinder

hammer

firing pin

barrel

frame

trigger mechanism

trigger guard

mainspring

hand grip

hammer

cartridge

Charles Darwin

In 1831 Charles Darwin set sail on HMS *Beagle*; during the voyage he made many observations that were eventually to prompt him to propose the theory of evolution through natural selection. Surprisingly, he did not ship aboard as a naturalist or biologist, but as a dinner companion for the captain.

Charles Darwin (1809–82) was the grandson of English physician Erasmus Darwin (1731–1802), whose only contribution to the theory of evolution was to support the (erroneous) ideas of French naturalist Jean-Baptiste Lamarck (1744–1829). When he was 22 years old, Charles Darwin joined HMS *Beagle* as company for the captain, Robert Fitzroy. Conventions of the time forbade the captain to socialize with officers or crew.

An unmissable opportunity

But Darwin also wanted to be a naturalist, and he used the five-year voyage as a unique opportunity to study the plants and animals from the farflung places he saw. The ship visited Tenerife and the Cape Verde Islands off the west coast of Africa before sailing around Cape Horn and up the western coast of South America. It then called at Patagonia, Chile, Peru, and the Galápagos Islands before sailing across the Pacific to Tahiti and New Zealand, returning to England by way of Mauritius and South Africa. At each port of call Darwin made observations and collected specimens.

Darwin made more trips ashore in South America than anywhere else on the five-year voyage—in fact, he spent more time on land than on the ship. In addition to exotic plants and animals, he also studied the rocks and geology of the places he visited. In Patagonia he came upon a shore with a 19.6-foot-high (6-m) gravel cliff containing some huge bones. They were too large to belong to any living creature, including the new

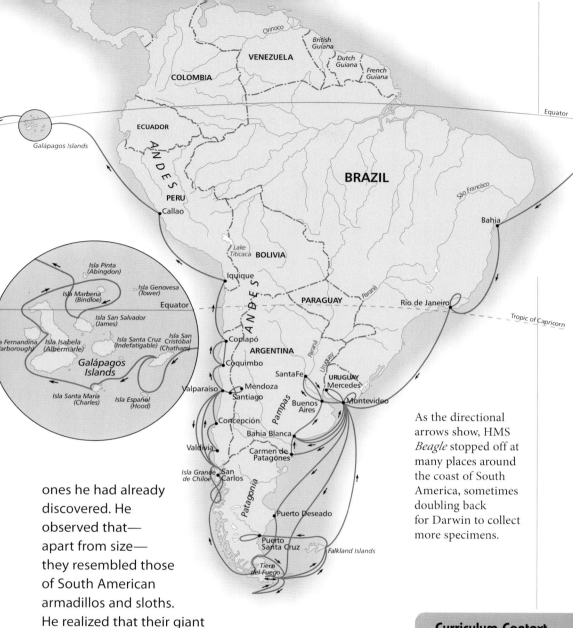

As the directional arrows show, HMS *Beagle* stopped off at many places around the coast of South America, sometimes doubling back for Darwin to collect more specimens.

ones he had already discovered. He observed that—apart from size—they resembled those of South American armadillos and sloths. He realized that their giant ancestors had become extinct, but what was it that had caused them to die out? It was as if they were not fit enough to survive.

Back home

The *Beagle* returned to England in the fall of 1836, and Darwin went to live in London. He studied geology and was converted to the uniformitarian ideas of

Curriculum Context

The curriculum requires that students read and understand scientists' original accounts, such as Darwin's *Voyage of the Beagle*.

Natural selection

The process in nature by which only the organisms best adapted to their environment tend to survive and transmit their genetic characteristics to succeeding generations, while those less adapted tend to be eliminated.

Scottish geologist Charles Lyell (1797–1875), who argued that the world was in a constant state of change. He also read the works of English economist Thomas Malthus (1766–1834), who described the "struggle for existence." Darwin recognized a similar state among animal species—why do some fish, for example, produce so many offspring when there is insufficient food for all of them? But some do survive, and this gave rise to Darwin's idea that only the fittest animals survive, and that a process of natural selection made some more fit than others.

At the same time as Darwin was putting together these ideas on evolution, Welsh naturalist Alfred Russel Wallace (1823–1913) came to very similar conclusions based on his observations of Asian and Australasian animals. He wrote of his theories in 1858, and sent a copy to Darwin. Immediately they consulted, and issued a joint paper to the Linnean Society, and Darwin finally finished his epic work *On the Origin of Species by Means of Natural Selection*, which was published the following year. In 1889, Wallace produced his own book on the subject of natural selection.

The science of genetics

Darwin's theory was that evolution takes place in stages by chance mutations. Favorable mutations are inherited and passed on to offspring, so producing a gradual change in a whole species. Eventually new, fitter species come into existence and old, less fit ones, become extinct. Of course Charles Darwin and his contemporaries had no idea exactly how mutations take place. But unknown to them, heredity was being studied in the garden of a monastery in Austria by the obscure monk Gregor Mendel (1822–84). He grew successive generations of pea plants, and figured out the basic laws of heredity—that offspring receive sets of inherited "factors" that we now call genes. Genetics provides the means by which evolution takes place.

Curriculum Context

Students should realize that advances, such as the theory of biological evolution, have important and long-lasting effects on science and society.

The Finches of the Galápagos Islands

The Galápagos are a group of volcanic islands about 620 miles (1,000 km) off the coast of Ecuador, South America. When HMS *Beagle* arrived there in September 1835, Darwin collected samples of the animals and birds, among them several species of finches. After he returned to England, ornithologist John Gould (1804–81) pointed out that many of the birds differed only in coloration and the shapes of their beaks. For example, the finches that fed on seeds had short, stubby beaks, while birds that fed on insects had long, thin beaks. Darwin deduced that they were all variations of a single species that lived originally on the mainland. When they arrived on the Galápagos, there were no other birds there to compete with, so they began to specialize in terms of diet. Some fed mainly on grubs, others on flying insects, and others on nuts, seeds, and so on. Gradually they evolved beaks appropriate to their chosen food. They interbred only with their own kind, and eventually evolved into separate species.

Of the 13 species of finches on the Galápagos Islands, eight very similar ones are known as Darwin's finches. Finches 1, 3, and 4 have relatively long beaks adapted for eating insects; finch 2 is a fruit-eating species; and the slightly crossed, stubby beaks of finches 5 and 6 are best at tackling seeds.

The two larger birds are ground finches, with powerful beaks for eating cacti. The small bird is a warbler finch, so called because of its resemblance to a warbler. It also lives on the Galápagos Islands and specializes in eating small insects.

Steamships

Following the production of a reliable steam engine by James Watt (1736–1819), some inventors experimented with an engine on wheels to make a steam locomotive, while others tried to use the engine as motive power for a boat. The idea seemed simple—just connect a steam engine to a paddle or paddles—but there were many failures before success was finally achieved in 1807.

Serious attempts to build a steamboat were first made in the late 18th century. In France, inventor Jacques Perrier tested an experimental craft on the Seine River in Paris in 1775, and in 1783 the French engineer Claude Jouffroy d'Abbans (1751–1832) constructed a 198-ton (180-tonne) steam paddleboat called *Pyroscaphe*, which was driven by a paddle at the back of the ship. Although others soon copied his idea, these ships were too small to be practical, and they were unsuited to rough open seas.

Other designs

Starting in 1785, American inventor John Fitch (1743–98) built models, and then full-sized boats, that used the engine to operate mechanical oars. He conducted the first steamboat trial on the Delaware River in 1787. All his craft resembled boats with wheels, and none was completely successful. The same year American engineer James Rumsey (1743–92) took a different approach. His vessel used its steam engine to work a powerful pump that sucked in water at the front of the boat and forced it out at the rear. He tested his water-jet-propelled craft on the Potomac River.

The next steam-powered vessel to take to the water was built in Scotland in 1788. The engine was made by Scottish engineer William Symington (1763–1831). On Loch Dalswinton the boat reached a speed of over 6 miles per hour (9 km/h). Symington then took up the

challenge himself. In 1802, with financial help from Lord Dundas, a governor of the Scottish Forth and Clyde Canal Company, he built a steam tugboat, the *Charlotte Dundas*. It had a two-cylinder steam engine. During a demonstration on the Forth and Clyde Canal, it towed two large barges for 20 miles (32 km) at 3.4 miles per hour (5.5 km/h). However, it was alleged that wash from the relatively fast vessel damaged the canal banks, and after a few years Symington had to abandon the trials.

First passenger steamboats

We now turn to American engineer Robert Fulton (1765–1815), who built the first commercially successful steamboat. He had built experimental craft in France—in 1803 one of his boats ran at 4.3 miles per

The paddle wheeler *Britannia* leaving Boston Harbor. The ship, launched in 1840, used wind power from sails as well as her steam-driven paddles.

hour (7 km/h) along the Seine River. But he returned to the United States in 1806 to design the *Clermont*, which was built in New York. In 1807, it made the trip along the Hudson River from New York to Albany at a speed of 5 miles per hour (8 km/h), and went into regular passenger service. In 1808, American engineer John Stevens (1749–1838) sailed his paddle steamer, the *Phoenix*, on the Delaware River, having sent it 150 miles (240 km) by sea from New York to Philadelphia.

Long-term success came in 1812 to a Scottish engineer. The 33-ton (30-tonne) *Comet*, built by Henry Bell (1767–1830), sailed along the Clyde River, and began a new age of steam navigation in Europe. The *Comet* ran a regular service from Glasgow to Helensburgh until it was wrecked in 1820. In 1814 American river captain Henry Shreve (1785–1851) built shallow-draft vessels

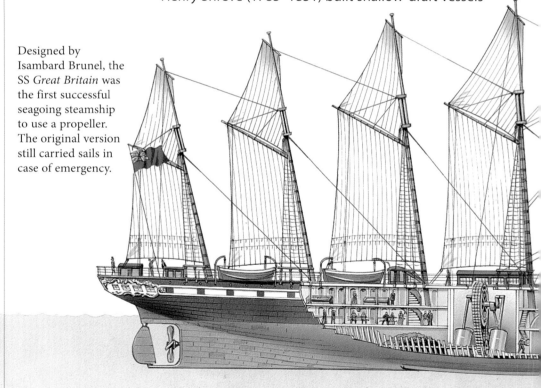

Designed by Isambard Brunel, the SS *Great Britain* was the first successful seagoing steamship to use a propeller. The original version still carried sails in case of emergency.

with a high-pressure steam engine mounted on deck, especially for traffic on the Mississippi and Ohio rivers. In the following year, Fulton launched the *Demologos* (or *Fulton the First*), a coastal defense vessel, and the world's first steam warship.

Crossing the Atlantic

By 1838, English engineer Isambard Brunel (1806–59) was building seagoing paddle steamers. The first Atlantic crossing using steam power alone was made in 1838, when two rival British steamship companies sent ships to New York. Brunel's ship, the *Great Western*, made the trip in 14 days, arriving a few hours after *Sirius*, which had left England four days before it. They were followed by propeller-driven ships such

Steam engine

An engine that converts the heat energy of pressurized steam into mechanical energy.

Propeller

A device for propelling a boat, consisting of a power-driven shaft with radiating blades that produces thrust when spinning.

The Screw Propeller

Although John Ericsson had invented the screw propeller in 1836, and fitted it to the U.S. warship *Princeton* in 1843, navies around the world were reluctant to adopt it. It was argued that although it was not as vulnerable as the paddle, it lacked the power needed to drive large ships. The argument was finally resolved in a dramatic manner in 1845. The British navy lashed the paddle wheeler *Alecto* and the screw propeller *Rattler* together in order to see which was the stronger. On April 3, in the North Sea the contest began. Initially, there was little movement as each vessel increased the power. Then, slowly the *Rattler* inched forward, gathering speed until it was towing the 900-ton (815-tonne) *Alecto* backward at a speed of 2.5 knots (3 mph, or 4.5 km/h). There was no more argument over the power and superiority of the screw.

as SS *Great Britain*, which crossed the Atlantic in 1845. The steamship reigned supreme on the world's oceans until the development of marine diesel engines at the beginning of the 20th century.

Steam, iron, and steel

Because the paddle used to propel the ship was exposed and vulnerable to damage from enemy gunfire, steam warships were not used until the invention of the underwater screw propeller in 1836 by the English engineer Francis Pettit Smith (1808–74) and a former Swedish army officer, John Ericsson (1803–89). Ericsson built the first warship powered by a propeller in 1843, the USS *Princeton*. Steamships continued to have sails until the 1870s, but the increasing range and reliability of steam engines meant that the sail gradually vanished from warships.

Another impact of the Industrial Revolution was the invention of warships with iron and, later, steel hulls. The idea of using iron plates to protect the wooden hulls of ships had been used as early as the 1590s by the Korean navy. In 1859, the French built *Gloire*, which was the first warship with a wooden hull covered in iron; such ships were called ironclads. In 1860, the

British took the idea further when the *Warrior* became the first warship that had a hull made solely of iron. The *Warrior* was 480 ft (145 m) long and had a speed of 14 knots (17 mph, or 26 km/h).

Toward the modern battleship

In 1862, John Ericsson made another key contribution to the development of warships. With the launch of *Monitor* he changed the way guns were placed on warships. The vessel's guns were positioned in a rotating turret on the deck, which allowed them to fire at targets to the front and rear of the ship, not just the side. In 1872 Eric Reed combined a steam engine, a steel hull, and the massive firepower of 12.5-inch (30-cm) guns mounted in turrets by launching the 14,000-ton (12,700-tonne) *Devastation*—the first truly modern battleship. The size and power of battleships continued to grow in the first half of the 20th century. However, the effectiveness of these huge warships was undermined by the rise of military air power, and by the start of World War II (1939–45). Warships became eclipsed by the aircraft carrier.

Designed by Dupuy de Lôme, the French frigate *Gloire* was the first warship to have its wooden hull protected by a layer of iron. This covering stretched from a point 6 ft (nearly 2 m) below the waterline to the upper deck, and was 4.75 in (12 cm) thick. The layer was completed by a 26 in (66 cm) oak backing.

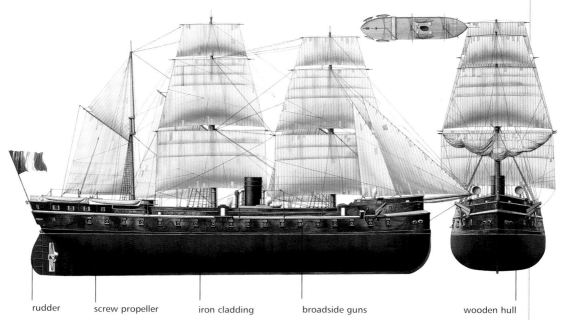

rudder   screw propeller   iron cladding   broadside guns   wooden hull

Timelines 1625–1659

Technology

1626 St. Peter's Basilica in Rome is finally consecrated, having taken 120 years to build; for over 250 years it stands as the world's largest Christian church.

1629 Italian engineer Giovanni Branca (1571–1640) makes a primitive steam turbine.

1631 French mathematician Pierre Vernier (1580–1637) invents the vernier measuring scale, which allows precise measurements to be made.

1641 Italian inventor Vincenzo Galilei (1606–49) tries (but fails) to make a pendulum clock, using a design produced by his father, Galileo Galilei (1564–1642).

1642 German engraver Ludwig von Siegen (1609–c.1680) devises the mezzotint process, in which effects of light and shade are produced by scraping away parts of a roughened metal printing plate.

1646 German scholar and inventor Athanasius Kircher (1601–80) describes a magic lantern that projects hand-drawn images.

1647 French scientist Blaise Pascal (1623–62) invents a primitive version of the roulette wheel to test his ideas on probability.

1650 German inventor Stephen Farfler constructs a three-wheeled invalid chair.

Biology and Medicine

1628 English physician William Harvey (1578–1657) explains the circulation of blood—the way in which blood is pumped by the heart through the lungs and around the rest of the body.

1642 German anatomist Johann Wirsung (1600–43) discovers the pancreatic duct, which carries digestive juices from the pancreas to the duodenum (part of the small intestine).

1649 English physician Henry Power (1623–68) discovers the extremely narrow capillary blood vessels.

Physical Sciences and Math

1627 German astronomer Johannes Kepler (1571–1630) publishes tables describing the motions of the planets; they become known as the Rudolphine Tables for the deceased Emperor Rudolph II, who funded their publication.

1633 Italian scientist Galileo Galilei (1564–1642) is condemned by the Roman Catholic Inquisition for refusing to withdraw his statement that the Sun—and not the Earth—is at the center of the Universe (which is against the teachings of the church at the time). Galileo is sentenced to house arrest in Florence.

1639 English astronomers William Crabtree (1610–44) and Jeremiah Horrocks (1617–41) make the first observation of the transit of the planet Venus across the Sun's disk.

1642 French scientist Blaise Pascal (1623–62) puts forward Pascal's law, which states that the pressure within a liquid is the same everywhere. The principle underlies the working of all hydraulic machinery, and the reason why it is possible to squeeze toothpaste from the end of a tube.

1645 Flemish cartographer Michael Langrenus (1600–75) publishes the first map of the Moon.

1652 Dutch hydraulic engineer Cornelius Vermuyden (1595–c.1683) completes the drainage of a large area of the Fens—the low marshy lands in the east of England—making them suitable for growing farm crops.

1654 German physicist Otto von Guericke (1602–86) of Magdeburg invents an air pump (which is the name given at that time to a vacuum pump). He gives a demonstration, and removes the air from between two copper hemispheres. Two teams of horses fail to pull it apart. The hemispheres, which become known as the Magdeburg spheres, are held together by atmospheric pressure.

1654 The Grand Duke of Tuscany, Ferdinand II (1610–70), makes a closed-ended thermometer (previous versions of liquid-in-glass thermometers had one end open, and had to be very long).

1656 Dutch scientist Christiaan Huygens (1629–95) designs a pendulum clock. His chronometer for use at sea, which he invents in 1659, fails to keep accurate time.

1658 English scientist Robert Hooke (1635–1703) makes a watch regulated by a hairspring (the power from the main spring of the watch is released very gradually, controlled by the oscillations of the hairspring).

1658 Dutch naturalist Jan Swammerdam (1637–80) describes red blood cells (erythrocytes).

1659 Italian anatomist Marcello Malpighi (1628–94) discovers the lymph nodes, enlarged structures where lymph vessels come together. Two years later he confirms the existence of capillary blood vessels.

1646 English scientist Thomas Browne (1605–82) coins the word "electricity" (which at that time was limited to static electricity).

1646 French scientist Blaise Pascal (1623–62) demonstrates the existence of atmospheric pressure, and confirms that it varies with altitude.

1650 The first properly equipped chemistry laboratory is established at the University of Leyden (now Leiden) in the Netherlands.

1650 German inventor Stephen Farfler constructs a three-wheeled invalid chair.

1655 Dutch scientist Christiaan Huygens (1629–95) uses a homemade telescope to observe the rings around the planet Saturn. He also discovers Titan, the largest of Saturn's moons.

1657 Dutch scientist Christiaan Huygens (1629–95) writes the first book on mathematical probability.

1659 German mathematician Johann Rahn (1622–76) introduces the division sign (÷) to mathematics.

Timelines 1660–1689

Technology

1660 English scientist Robert Hooke (1635–1703) devises the anchor escapement to regulate a pendulum-driven clock.

1661 Dutch scientist Christiaan Huygens (1629–95) invents the manometer, a device for measuring gas pressure.

1663 Scottish mathematician and inventor James Gregory (1638–75) proposes a design for a reflecting telescope.

1664 Italian engineer Giuseppe Campani (1635–1715) creates a lens-grinding lathe (for making lenses for optical instruments).

1666 French engineer Jean de Thévenot (1620–92) makes the spirit level.

1667 English scientist Robert Hooke (1635–1703) invents the anemometer, an instrument for measuring wind speed. It is later to have important applications in the study of weather.

1668 English scientist and mathematician Isaac Newton (1642–1727) builds a reflecting telescope.

1670 French winemaker Dom Pérignon (1638–1715) creates champagne.

1674 English glassmaker George Ravenscroft (1618–81) develops lead crystal glass.

1674 The military engineer Menno von Coehoorn (1641–1704) invents the trench mortar.

Biology and Medicine

1665 English scientist Robert Hooke (1635–1703) coins the word "cell" to describe the "little boxes" he observes in plant tissues, using a compound microscope of his own invention.

1669 Dutch naturalist Jan Swammerdam (1637–80) describes metamorphosis in insects—the sequence of changes from egg to larva to pupa to adult.

1676 Dutch scientist Antonie van Leeuwenhoek (1632–1723) reports his observations of bacteria, using a simple microscope made with lenses he ground himself. A year later, he observes human sperm.

1681 On the Indian Ocean island of Mauritius, the dodo (*Raphus cucullatus*), a large flightless bird of the pigeon family, becomes extinct.

Physical Sciences and Math

1661 Irish scientist Robert Boyle (1627–91) publishes his book *The Sceptical Chymist*, in which he defines chemical elements for the first time. A year later, he formulates Boyle's law, which states that at a fixed temperature the pressure of a gas is inversely proportional to its volume.

1664 English scientist Robert Hooke (1635–1703) describes Jupiter's Great Red Spot (a major feature of Jupiter's surface now known to be due to a gigantic storm in the atmosphere). In the same year, Hooke proposes that the planets are held in their orbits by the force of gravity between them and the Sun.

1665 English scientist Robert Hooke (1635–1703) proposes the wave theory of light, but his proposal is largely ignored until championed by Christiaan Huygens in 1678.

1671 English scientist Isaac Newton (1642–1727) demonstrates that a glass prism splits white light into a spectrum of rainbow colors—the phenomenon known as dispersion of light.

1675 English scientist Isaac Newton (1642–1727) proposes the corpuscular theory of light: that light travels as a series of rapidly moving minute particles. He does not publish his theory until 1704.

1675   Dutch scientist Christiaan Huygens (1629–95) invents the oscillating balance and hairspring regulator for clocks.

1675   English watchmaker Thomas Tompion (1639–1713) makes a watch with a hairspring escapement.

1675   Irish scientist Robert Boyle (1627–91) devises a hydrometer (an instrument for measuring the relative density of a liquid). It soon finds important applications in science and industry.

1676   English scientist Robert Hooke (1635–1703) invents the universal joint (for connecting two driven shafts joined at an angle).

1679   French physicist Denis Papin (1647–1712) produces a steam digester, the forerunner of the pressure cooker.

1680   English clockmaker Daniel Quare (1648–1724) makes a repeating watch that chimes the hours.

1680   Irish scientist Robert Boyle (1627–91) invents a match that uses a mixture of sulfur and phosphorus. It remained the basic "strike anywhere" match for more than 200 years.

1687   French physicist Guillaume Amontons (1663–1705) invents a hygrometer (an instrument for measuring humidity).

1689   German Johann Denner (1655–1707) develops the clarinet (as a single-reed instrument with no keys).

1682   English botanist Nehemiah Grew (1641–1712) decribes the male and female parts of flowers.

1683   English physician Thomas Sydenham (1624–89) gives the first full description of gout.

1683   The wild boar (*Sus scrofa*) becomes extinct in the British Isles.

1686   English naturalist John Ray (1627–1705) proposes the word "species" to describe an interbreeding group of plants.

1676   Danish astronomer Ole Rømer (1644–1710) measures (inaccurately) the speed of light.

1678   Dutch scientist Christiaan Huygens (1629–95) takes up the wave theory of light proposed by English scientist Robert Hooke (1635–1703) in 1665: that light travels as a series of minute waves.

1679   German mathematician Gottfried Leibniz (1646–1716) introduces binary arithmetic, which uses only two digits. Today it is employed by all computers.

1679   English scientist Robert Hooke (1635–1703) proposes the inverse square law of gravity.

1682   English astronomer Edmond Halley (1656–1742) plots the course of Halley's comet. In 1705, he correctly predicts that it will return in 1758.

1684   Italian astronomer Giovanni Cassini (1625–1712) discovers Dione and Thetys, two of Saturn's moons.

1687   English scientist and mathematician Isaac Newton (1642–1727) publishes his major work *Principia*, in which he sets out his various theories in astronomy, mathematics, and physics.

Technology

1690 French engineer Denis Papin (1647–1712) conceives the idea of a steam-powered paddleboat, and constructs a primitive steam engine.

1694 English clockmaker Daniel Quare (1648–1724) makes a portable barometer.

1698 English engineer Henry Winstanley (1644–1703) completes the first lighthouse at Eddystone Rocks in the English Channel; in 1699, the height was increased because ocean spray was extinguishing the light.

1698 English mining engineer Thomas Savery (c.1650–1715) invents a steam pump, which becomes the forerunner of the atmospheric steam engine.

1700 Swedish engineer Christoph Polhem (1661–1751) improves metal rolling mills to produce bars with shaped profiles.

1701 English agriculturist Jethro Tull (1674–1741) invents a mechanical seed drill for sowing seeds.

1703 The first Eddystone lighthouse is swept away in a violent storm. Winstanley achieved his wish of being in the lighthouse as it faced the strongest storm, and died as a result.

1703 English physicist Francis Hawksbee (c.1666–1713) invents an improved vacuum pump.

1704 Italian clockmaker Nicolas Fatio de Duiller (1664–1753) makes a clock with jewel bearings.

Biology and Medicine

1694 German botanist Rudolf Camerarius (1665–1721) establishes the existence of male and female sexes in plants.

1696 Dutch scientist Antonie van Leeuwenhoek (1632–1723) publishes a description of microorganisms (which he called "animalcules"); today we know most of them as protists.

1701 Italian physician Giacomo Pylarini (1659–1715) inoculates three children in Constantinople with smallpox to prevent more serious disease when they are older; some people consider Pylarini to be the first immunologist.

Physical Sciences and Math

1694 Italian scientist Carlo Renaldini (1615–98) suggests that both the freezing point and boiling point of water should be used as "fixed points" on thermometers.

1697 German chemist Georg Stahl (1660–1734) champions the (incorrect) phlogiston theory of combustion devised by Johann Becher (1635–82) in 1669.

1704 English scientist and mathematician Isaac Newton (1642–1727) publishes his book *Opticks*, in which he champions the corpuscular (particle) theory of light, and explains the actions of lenses and prisms.

1709 English physicist Francis Hawksbee (c.1666–1713) describes capillary action, the phenomenon that causes a liquid to rise up a very narrow tube, and a sponge or blotting paper to soak up liquids.

1712 Italian mathematician Giovanni Ceva (c.1647–c.1734) publishes *De Re Numeraria* (Concerning Money Matters), the first clear application of math to economics.

1706 English physicist Francis Hawksbee (*c.*1666–1713) constructs an electrostatic generator.

1709 English iron founder Abraham Darby (*c.*1678–1717) introduces the use of coke for iron smelting (previously only expensive charcoal could be used).

1709 Polish-born Dutch physicist Gabriel Fahrenheit (1686–1736) invents the alcohol thermometer, and the Fahrenheit temperature scale.

1712 English engineer Thomas Newcomen (1663–1729) invents an atmospheric steam engine that employs a piston, unlike the engine built by Thomas Savery (*c.*1650–1715) in 1698.

1714 The British government offers a prize of £20,000 to the person who devises a method of finding longitude accurately at sea. In 1759, English clockmaker John Harrison (1693–1776) claims the prize, but has to wait 14 years to be paid in full.

1715 English clockmaker John Harrison (1693–1776) invents a clock that runs for eight days on a single winding.

1716 English astronomer Edmond Halley (1656–1742) invents the diving bell, so that workmen can build foundations underwater.

1718 English inventor James Puckle patents a flintlock semi-automatic cannon.

1707 English physician John Floyer (1649–1734) produces a special watch for counting patients' pulse rates.

1711 Italian naturalist Luigi Marsigli (1658–1730) shows the animal nature of corals (formerly held to be plants).

1717 Italian physician Giovanni Lancisi (1654–1720) blames malaria on the bite of the mosquito in his book *De Noxiis Paludum Effluviis* (Concerning the Noxious Effluvia of Marshes).

1717 English astronomer Abraham Sharp (1651–1742) calculates the value of π (pi) to 72 decimal places.

1718 English astronomer Edmond Halley (1656–1742) identifies stellar proper motion, which is the apparent movement of a star on the celestial sphere. It results from the star's very gradual movement relative to the Sun (not relative to the Earth). Stars with the largest proper motions are closest to the Earth.

1718 French astronomer Jacques Cassini (1677–1756), in a joint publication with his father Giovanni Cassini (1625–1712), confirms Descartes's (incorrect) prediction that the Earth is elongated at the poles.

1718 French mathematician Abraham de Moivre (1667–1754) produces *The Doctrine of Chances*, his first book on probability.

1719 English mathematician Brook Taylor (1685–1731) publishes *New Principles of Linear Perspective*, in which he demonstrates the principle of the vanishing point.

Technology

c.1720 English clockmaker Christopher Pinchbeck (c.1670–1732) produces the copper–zinc alloy pinchbeck. It resembles gold, and it is used widely in making watches and jewelry.

1725 Scottish goldsmith William Ged (1690–1749) introduces stereotype printing, in which a mold is cast from a complete page of type, and used to make a printing plate.

1726 English inventor George Graham (1673–1751) invents the mercury pendulum for clocks, which does not change in length with changes in temperature.

1728 English clockmaker John Harrison (1693–1776) creates the gridiron pendulum for clocks. Like George Graham's invention, its length is not affected by variations in temperature.

1728 French dentist Pierre Fauchard (1678–1761) invents the first dental drill and introduces tooth fillings.

1730 English mathematician John Hadley (1682–1744) devises the quadrant, a navigational instrument that was the forerunner of the sextant. A year later (1731), he produces an improved instrument called the octant.

1732 French physicist Henri Pitot (1695–1771) creates the Pitot tube, an instrument for measuring speed of air flow. In the 20th century it is used as an air-speed indicator for aircraft.

1733 English engineer John Kay (1704–64) patents the flying shuttle, which greatly increases the speed at which a loom makes cloth.

Biology and Medicine

1721 American physician Zabdiel Boylston (1676–1766) carries out the first smallpox inoculation in the United States.

1728 The first botanical garden in the United States is opened by naturalist and explorer John Bartram (1699–1777) at his home near Philadelphia.

1731 English agriculturist Jethro Tull (1674–1741) publishes *The New Horse-Hoeing Husbandry*, a book that recommends harrowing the soil, growing crops in rows, removing weeds by hoeing, and using manure as fertilizer.

1735 Swedish naturalist Carolus Linnaeus (1707–78) publishes *Systema Naturae.*

Physical Sciences and Math

1724 Dutch scientist Hermann Boerhaave (1668–1738) publishes his book *Elementa Chemiae* (Elements of Chemistry), the first major chemistry textbook.

1725 German physician Johann Schulze (1684–1744) observes that daylight turns certain silver salts dark (later to have significance in photography).

1729 English physicist Stephen Gray (1666–1736) distinguishes between electrical insulators and conductors.

1731 English astronomer John Bevis (1695–1771) discovers the Crab Nebula.

1735 English physicist Stephen Gray (1666–1736) postulates that lightning is an electrical phenomenon.

1736 French surveyor Alexis Clairaut (1713–65) measures the length of 1 degree of meridian (longitude), thus enabling accurate calculation of the size of the Earth.

1737 Swedish chemist Georg Brandt (1694–1768) discovers cobalt, the first discovery of a completely new metal since ancient times.

1733 English amateur astronomer Chester Hall (1703–71) develops a simple achromatic lens for telescopes. (An achromatic lens does not produce colored fringes around the image.)

1735 English clockmaker John Harrison (1693–1776) unveils his first chronometer, a clock that keeps time well enough to be used to calculate longitude at sea.

1738 English inventor Lewis Paul (d.1759) produces a machine for carding wool. With English engineer John Wyatt (1700–66), Paul went on to invent a water-powered spinning machine.

1740 English metallurgist Benjamin Huntsman (1704–76) invents the crucible process for making steel in batches.

1742 American scientist and politician Benjamin Franklin (1706–90) invents a wood-burning stove. The design is patented, and later stoves of the same design come to be known as "Franklin stoves."

1742 French metallurgist Jean-Paul Malouin (1701–78) creates a process for covering steel with a layer of zinc (later to be called galvanizing).

1743 English metalworker Thomas Boulsover (1706–88) produces "Sheffield plate," metalware consisting of copper coated with a thin layer of silver.

1745 Dutch physicist Pieter van Musschenbroek (1692–1761) invents the Leyden jar, a simple form of electrical condenser.

1736 French explorer Charles-Marie de la Condamine (1701–74) discovers India rubber (then called caoutchouc).

1745 French surgeon Jacques Daviel (1693–1762) successfully performs an operation for the removal of a cataract from a patient's eye.

1747 Scottish physician James Lind (1716–94) experiments with citrus fruits to prevent scurvy among sailors in the British Royal Navy.

1748 Scottish physician John Fothergill (1712–80) gives the first description of diphtheria.

1742 Swedish astronomer Anders Celsius (1701–44) devises the 100-degree Celsius temperature scale (later known as the centigrade scale, but now called by its original name).

1743 French mathematician Jean d'Alembert (1717–83) establishes mathematical dynamics (a branch of mechanics) with his book *Traité de Dynamique* (Treatise on Dynamics).

1743 English mathematician Thomas Simpson (1710–61) devises Simpson's rules, a systematic approach to finding the area bounded by a curve.

1745 Russian scientist Mikhail Lomonosov (1711–65) compiles a catalog of more than 300 minerals.

1747 German chemist Andreas Marggraf (1709–82) discovers sugar in beets.

1748 English astronomer James Bradley (1693–1762) discovers the nutation of the Earth, which is the slight "nodding" of the Earth's axis as it describes a very slow circle in space.

Timelines 1750–1783

Technology

1750 German engineer Johann Segner (1704–77) constructs a reaction waterwheel.

1757 English clockmaker Thomas Mudge (1715–94) devises a lever escapement for a watch.

1758 English cotton weaver Jedediah Strutt (1726–97) invents the stocking frame, a machine for making ribbed hosiery.

1758 English optician John Dollond (1706–61) makes achromatic lenses that consist of two pieces of different glass types (crown glass and flint glass).

1761 English engineer James Brindley (1716–72) completes the construction of the Bridgewater Canal.

1762 English nobleman John Montagu, earl of Sandwich (1718–92), invents the sandwich.

1764 English mechanic James Hargreaves (d. 1778) invents the spinning jenny for spinning many cotton or woolen threads at once.

1765 Scottish engineer James Watt (1736–1819) builds a steam engine with a separate condenser.

***c.*1769** English engineer John Smeaton (1724–92) designs a cylinder-boring machine.

1769 French military engineer Nicolas-Joseph Cugnot (1725–1804) builds a steam-powered three-wheel vehicle (for towing guns).

1770 English chemist Joseph Priestley (1733–1804) invents the pencil eraser.

Biology and Medicine

1752 French chemist René-Antoine Ferchault de Réaumur (1683–1757) discovers the part played by gastric juices in the digestion of foods.

1760s English agriculturist Robert Bakewell (1725–95) uses selective breeding to produce improved varieties of farm animals.

1762 The flightless dodolike bird called the solitaire (*Pezophaps solitaria*) becomes extinct (on Rodriguez Island in the Indian Ocean).

1763 German botanist Josef Kölreuter (1733–1806) discovers the role of insects in the pollination of flowers.

Physical Sciences and Math

1752 American Benjamin Franklin (1706–90) demonstrates the electrical nature of lightning with a kite-flying experiment.

1758 German astronomer Johann Palitzsch (1723–88) observes Halley's comet when it returns as predicted by English astronomer Edmond Halley (1656–1742) in 1682.

1761 Scottish chemist Joseph Black (1728–99) introduces the concept of latent heat.

1761 Russian scientist Mikhail Lomonosov (1711–65) observes a transit of Venus across the Sun's disk, and deduces that Venus has an atmosphere.

1766 English scientist Henry Cavendish (1731–1810) identifies hydrogen, which he calls "inflammable air."

1767 Swiss mathematician Leonhard Euler (1707–83) sets out the rules of algebra in his book *Vollständige Anleitung zur Algebra* (Complete Instruction in Algebra).

1772 Scottish chemist Daniel Rutherford (1749–1819) discovers nitrogen.

1772 Swedish chemist Karl Scheele (1742–86) discovers oxygen, but does not publish his findings until 1777.

1770 French watchmaker Abraham-Louis Perrelet (1729–1826) develops a watch with automatic winding.

1774 English engineer John Wilkinson (1728–1808) patents a precision cannon-boring machine, also used for making cylinders for steam engines.

1776 American inventor David Bushnell (c.1742–1824) builds the *Turtle*, one of the first submarines.

1777 French physicist Charles Coulomb (1736–1806) invents the torsion balance, a sensitive instrument for measuring electrical, magnetic, and gravitational forces.

1778 English inventor Joseph Bramah (1748–1814) patents a flushing toilet that uses a ball valve and a siphon (like the usual modern system).

1779 English weaver Samuel Crompton (1753–1827) builds the spinning mule, a machine that twists multiple strands of fibers to form individual lengths of yarn, and winds them onto bobbins.

1783 Two French brothers, Joseph (1740–1810) and Jacques (1745–99) Montgolfier, invent the hot-air balloon.

1783 French physicist Jacques-Alexandre Charles (1746–1823) invents the hydrogen-filled balloon.

Technology

1778 German-born physician Friedrich (or Franz) Mesmer (1734–1815) first practices in Paris a form of hypnotism that becomes known as mesmerism. Later (1785), he is denounced as a charlatan, and is unable to demonstrate any scientific basis for mesmerism.

1779 Dutch-born British scientist Jan Ingenhousz (1730–99) describes the process of photosynthesis in plants.

1780 American physician Benjamin Rush (1745–1813) describes dengue fever (then also known as breakbone fever).

Biology and Medicine

1774 English chemist Joseph Priestley (1733–1804) identifies oxygen and publishes his findings. In the same year he describes ammonia.

1774 French chemist Antoine Lavoisier (1743–94) demonstrates the law of conservation of mass (in a chemical reaction).

1776 English chemist Joseph Priestley (1733–1804) synthesizes nitrous oxide ("laughing gas"), later to be employed as an anesthetic in dentistry.

1778 Italian physicist Alessandro Volta (1745–1827) discovers methane.

1779 Swiss scientist Horace de Saussure (1740–99) coins the term "geology."

1781 French astronomer Charles Messier (1730–1817) publishes the Messier Catalog (of 100 or so nebulas, galaxies, etc.).

1783 English physicist John Michell (1724–93) predicts the existence of black holes, which he calls "dark stars."

Physical Sciences and Math

Technology

1784 American scientist and politician Benjamin Franklin (1706–90) invents bifocal eyeglasses.

1785 English inventor Edmund Cartwright (1743–1823) makes a steam-powered loom.

1785 French balloonist Jean-Pierre Blanchard (1753–1809) invents the parachute.

1786 Scottish millwright and inventor Andrew Meikle (1719–1811) makes a threshing machine (patented 1788).

1787 English engineer John Wilkinson (1728–1808) builds an iron-hulled boat.

1788 Scottish banker Patrick Miller (1731–1815) and Scottish engineer William Symington (1763–1831) build a steam paddleboat.

1790 Two French brothers, Claude (1763–1805) and Ignace (1760–1829) Chappe, invent an optical telegraph.

1792 Scottish engineer William Murdock (1754–1839) introduces domestic lighting using coal gas.

1793 American engineer Eli Whitney (1765–1825) invents the cotton gin.

1793 French balloonist Jean-Pierre Blanchard (1753–1809) makes the first untethered hot-air balloon flight to take place in the U. S.

1795 English inventor Joseph Bramah (1748–1814) invents a hydraulic press.

1797 American engineer Charles Newbold (b. 1780) patents a cast-iron plow.

Biology and Medicine

1785 English physician William Withering (1741–99) introduces the use of the drug digitalis, made from the foxglove plant, to treat dropsy (fluid retention due to heart disease). The drug is used today for certain heart disorders.

1789 English naturalist and clergyman Gilbert White (1720–93) publishes *The Natural History and Antiquities of Selborne*, a detailed year-long study of the habits of local animals, which is still read by naturalists today.

Physical Sciences and Math

1784 English scientist Henry Cavendish (1731–1810) proves that water is a compound (of hydrogen and oxygen, H_2O) and not an element. A year later he also determines the composition of nitric acid (HNO_3).

1787 German-born English astronomer William Herschel (1738–1822) observes Oberon and Titania, two moons of the planet Uranus (which he had discovered in 1781). Two years later he discovers Saturn's moons Enceladus and Mimas, and in 1790 he identifies the first planetary nebula.

***c*.1787** French physicist Jacques-Alexandre Charles (1746–1823) postulates Charles's law: that, at constant pressure, the volume of a gas is proportional to its absolute temperature.

1788 French mathematician Joseph Lagrange (1736–1813) publishes his book *Mécanique Analytique*, which deals with the calculus of mechanics.

1795 French astronomer Joseph de Lalande (1732–1807) records observations of Neptune, but he does not recognize it as a new planet.

1800 Italian physicist Alessandro Volta (1745–1827) invents the voltaic pile battery for producing a continuous electric current.

1801 English engineer Richard Trevithick (1771–1833) constructs a steam-powered road "locomotive." In 1803, he builds the first successful steam railroad locomotive.

1801 American chemist Robert Hare (1781–1858) invents an oxyhydrogen blowpipe that can produce flames of extremely high temperature.

1802 Scottish engineer William Symington (1763–1831) builds one of the most successful early steamboats, the *Charlotte Dundas*.

1804 English inventor and founder of the science of aerodynamics George Cayley (1773–1857) builds and flies a model glider.

1805 French inventor Joseph Jacquard (1752–1834) constructs a loom that is controlled by a "chain" of punched cards.

1806 English military engineer William Congreve (1772–1828) constructs solid-fuel rockets.

1807 American engineer Robert Fulton (1765–1815) builds a successful paddle steamer, *Clermont* (originally the North River Steam Boat).

1794 English chemist John Dalton (1766–1844) describes color blindness, a condition from which he and his brother both suffer.

1796 English physician Edward Jenner (1749–1823) introduces smallpox vaccination in Europe.

1802 French naturalist Jean-Baptiste Lamarck (1744–1829) introduces the word "biology" for the study of living things and life processes.

1803 German physician John Otto (1774–1844) describes the inherited blood disorder hemophilia.

1798 American-born British scientist and administrator Benjamin Thompson, Count Rumford (1753–1814), establishes the beginnings of the modern theory that heat is a form of motion.

1799 Benjamin Thompson helps found the Royal Institution in London.

1800 English astronomer William Herschel (1738–1822) discovers infrared radiation (from the Sun).

1801 English physicist Thomas Young (1773–1829) observes the interference of light.

1801 English chemist John Dalton (1766–1844) proposes the law of partial pressures (sometimes called Dalton's law).

1801 French chemist Charles Désormes (1777–1862) establishes the formula for carbon dioxide (CO_2).

1801 German physicist Johann Ritter (1776–1810) discovers ultraviolet light.

1803 English chemist William Henry (1774–1836) formulates Henry's law.

1803 English chemist John Dalton (1766–1844) proposes his atomic theory.

Technology

1808 English chemist Humphry Davy (1778–1829) invents the arc lamp.

1808 English inventor George Cayley (1773–1857) builds a full-sized (unmanned) glider.

1808 American engineer John Stevens (1749–1838) builds the first steamboat to go to sea, the *Phoenix*.

1810 French chef Nicolas Appert (*c.*1750–1841) invents food canning (originally for Napoleon's army).

1812 English scientist William Wollaston (1766–1828) invents the camera lucida.

1813 English engineer William Hedley (1799–1843) builds his steam locomotive *Puffing Billy*.

1813 Swiss engineer Johann Bodmer (1786–1864) invents a breech-loading cannon.

1815 English chemist Humphry Davy (1778–1829) and English engineer George Stephenson (1781–1848) independently invent the miner's safety lamp.

1816 Scottish physicist David Brewster (1781–1868) invents the kaleidoscope.

1816 German engineer Karl Drais von Sauerbronn (1785–1851) builds the Draisienne—a steerable "hobby horse" resembling a primitive bicycle.

1816 German musician Johann Maelzel (1772–1838) patents the metronome, a clockwork upside-down pendulum that ticks to help students keep time with the music.

Biology and Medicine

1809 French naturalist Jean-Baptiste Lamarck (1744–1829) postulates that acquired characteristics (for example, a weightlifter's muscles) are inherited by offspring—a now discredited theory known as Lamarckism.

1811 Scottish anatomist Charles Bell (1774–1842) distinguishes between motor nerves (which are concerned with movement) and sensory nerves (which are concerned with sensations such as touch).

1817 French physician René Laënnec (1781–1826) uses a stethoscope—a single-tube device of his own design—to listen to a patient's heartbeat.

Physical Sciences and Math

1808 French physicist Étienne Malus (1775–1812) discovers the polarization of light by reflection from a mirror.

1808 French scientist Joseph Gay-Lussac (1778–1850) formulates Gay-Lussac's law.

1811 Italian scientist Amedeo Avogadro (1776–1856) posits Avogadro's law.

1811 German-born English astronomer William Herschel (1738–1822) proposes a theory that stars develop from nebulas as clouds of gas condense into star clusters.

1815 English chemist William Prout (1785–1850) proposes that the atomic weights of all elements are exact multiples of the atomic weight of hydrogen.

1815 English scholar Peter Roget (1779–1869) devises a slide rule with two logarithmic scales, which greatly simplifies multiplication and division.

1815 The explosion of Mount Tambora on the island of Sumbawa in Indonesia throws enough volcanic ash and dust into the atmosphere to temporarily modify climates throughout the world.

1817 Welsh engineer Richard Roberts (1789–1864) invents a metal-planing machine.

1819 German inventor Augustus Siebe (1788–1872) develops a pressurized diving suit complete with helmet.

1822 American engineer William Church (c.1778–1863) patents a typesetting machine in England.

1823 Scottish chemist Charles Macintosh (1766–1843) patents waterproof fabric made by impregnating cloth with rubber.

1824 English mason Joseph Aspdin (1778–1855) patents Portland cement, made from a mixture of limestone and clay or limestone and shale.

1825 English physicist William Sturgeon (1783–1850) makes the first electromagnet.

1825 The Stockton & Darlington Railway, the first steam railroad to offer a regular service, opens in northern England. Its engineers are George Stephenson (1781–1848) and Robert Stephenson (1803–59).

1825 Scottish engineer Thomas Drummond (1797–1840) creates limelight (also called Drummond light), in which a piece of limestone is heated to incandescence in an oil or gas flame.

1822 French naturalist Jean-Baptiste Lamarck (1744–1829) distinguishes between vertebrates (animals with backbones) and invertebrates.

1823 The medical journal *The Lancet* is published for the first time in London.

1825 Scottish botanist David Douglas (1798–1834) discovers the Douglas fir in North America.

1825 French naturalist Georges Cuvier (1769–1832) puts forward his catastrophe theory of extinction.

1820 Danish physicist Hans Christian Ørsted (1777–1851) discovers electromagnetism by noticing the deflection of a compass needle in the magnetic field caused by an electric current flowing along a nearby wire.

1822 French physicist André-Marie Ampère (1775–1836) formulates the laws of electrodynamics that deal with electricity and magnetism.

1824 Swedish chemist Jöns Berzelius (1779–1848) discovers silicon; a year later Danish physicist Hans Christian Ørsted (1777–1851) prepares an impure form of aluminum.

1825 English chemist and physicist Michael Faraday (1791–1867) discovers benzene and several of its compounds.

1825 French chemist Michel Chevreul (1786–1889) discovers stearic acid, soon to be used widely in making candles.

Glossary

Boyle's Law At constant temperature, the absolute pressure and the volume of a gas are inversely proportional.

cast iron A hard, brittle form of iron that contains 2 to 4.5 percent carbon, which makes it very fluid when molten and easier to cast into complex shapes.

eclipse An alignment between the Sun and two other celestial objects in which one body blocks the Sun's light from the other.

fingerprint The individually unique ridges and patterns that appear on the ends of the fingers and thumbs.

flintlock A mechanism that ignites the charge in a muzzle-loading pistol or musket.

gravity The force of attraction existing between all matter in the Universe.

Industrial Revolution The change to industrial methods of production that began in the late 18th century.

lightning A discharge of atmospheric electricity, accompanied by a vivid flash of light, commonly from one cloud to another, sometimes from a cloud to the Earth.

mercury A heavy silvery metallic element, which is the only metal that is liquid at ordinary temperatures.

meridian An imaginary arc on the Earth's surface from the North Pole to the South Pole that connects all locations with a given longitude.

natural selection The process in nature by which only the organisms best adapted to their environment tend to survive and transmit their genetic characteristics to succeeding generations, while those less adapted tend to be eliminated.

ore A mineral or group of minerals from which a valuable constituent, especially a metal, can be profitably mined or extracted.

patent A grant made by a government that confers upon the creator of an invention the sole right to make, use, and sell that invention for a set period of time.

pendulum A body suspended from a fixed support so that it swings freely back and forth under the influence of gravity.

plow An apparatus pulled by an ox, horse, or modern tractor, that is used to cut, lift, and turn soil in farm fields.

polestar The star Polaris that lies nearly in a direct line with the axis of the Earth's rotation "above" the North Pole.

pressure The force per unit area acting on an object, measured in units such as atmospheres, bars, or pascals.

propeller A device for propelling a boat, consisting of a power-driven shaft with radiating blades that produces thrust.

reaper Any farm machine that cuts cereal crops in the field.

speed of light The speed of light in the vacuum of free space is an important physical constant equalling 186,288 miles (299,793 km) per second.

static electricity An accumulation of electric charge on an insulated body.

steam engine An engine that converts the heat energy of pressurized steam into mechanical energy.

steel A generally hard, strong, durable, malleable alloy of iron and carbon, usually containing between 0.2 and 1.5 percent carbon, often with other constituents.

tugboat A small powerful boat designed for towing or pushing larger vessels.

vacuum A completely empty space in which there are no atoms or molecules of any substance.

vernier An auxiliary device designed to allow fine adjustments or measurements.

Index

Words and page numbers in **bold** type indicate main references to the various topics. Page numbers in *italic* refer to illustrations. An asterisk before a page range indicates mentions on each page rather than unbroken discussion.